WORLD WAR I BATTLEFIELDS

A TRAVEL GUIDE TO THE WESTERN FRONT
SITES • MUSEUMS • MEMORIALS

EMMA THOMSON
JOHN RULER

www.bradtg

T0016955

Bradt Guides Ltd, UK
The Globe Pequot Press Inc, USA

Bradt GUIDES
TRAVEL TAKEN SERIOUSLY

AUTHORS

John Ruler is a Life Member of the British Guild of Travel Writers. He lives in Kent and is a specialist in Nord-Pas-de-Calais, writing about his cross-Channel neighbour for magazines and newspapers. He also writes about local history on both sides of the Channel.

Emma Thomson was named Travel Writer of the Year by the British Guild of Travel Writers in 2022 and 2019. She writes for national newspapers and magazines and is a regular contributor to BBC Radio Four's *From Our Own Correspondent*.

Third edition published November 2023
First published 2014

Bradt Guides Ltd
31a High Street, Chesham, Buckinghamshire, HP5 1BW, England
www.bradtguides.com
Print edition published in the USA by The Globe Pequot Press Inc,
PO Box 480, Guilford, Connecticut 06437-0480

Text copyright © 2023 Emma Thomson and John Ruler
Maps copyright © 2023 Bradt Guides Ltd; includes map data © OpenStreetMap contributors
Photographs copyright © 2023 Individual photographers (see below)
Project Manager: Elspeth Beidas
Cover research: Pepi Bluck, Perfect Picture

The author and publisher have made every effort to ensure the accuracy of the information in this book at the time of going to press. However, they cannot accept any responsibility for any loss, injury or inconvenience resulting from the use of information contained in this guide. All rights reserved. No part of this publication may be reproduced, stored in a retrieval system, or transmitted in any form or by any means, electronic, mechanical, photocopying, recording or otherwise without the prior consent of the publisher.

ISBN: 9781804691366

British Library Cataloguing in Publication Data
A catalogue record for this book is available from the British Library

Photographs @FortSeclin (@FS); Aisne Tourisme: ADRT02 (AD2/AT), FX Dessirier (FXD/AT); Alamy: Arterra Picture Library (APL/A), Sylvain CAMBON (SCa/A), STEVEN COTTAM (SCo/A), Chronicle (C/A), Flament/Andia (F/A/A), Paul Grove (PG/A), Allan Hartley (AH/A), ImagesEurope (IE/A), Tetyana Kochneva (TK/A); A.S.F.L. (Association Sauvegarde du Fort de Leveau) (ASFL); Pas-de-Calais Tourisme (PCT); Shutterstock: Nina Alizada (NA/S), Aqeela_Image (AI/S), Natalia Bratslavsky (NB/S), Paul Daniels (PD/S), Carrie Gomez (CG/S), Erik AJV (EA/S), Everett Collection (EC/S), Kev Gregory (KG/S), peter jeffreys (pj/S), Harald Lueder (HL/S), Jon Nicholls Photography (JNP/S), Willequet Manuel (WM/S), Pecold (P/S), Christopher Sharpe (CS/S), Todamo (T/S), Traveller70 (T70/S); Somme Tourisme (ST): AB (AB/ST), CarrierAude (CA/ST); SuperStock (SS); Emma Thomson (ET); Tourisme Grand Verdun: Cécile Thouvenin (CT/TGV); Visitflanders: Copper Tree Media Ltd UK (CTM/VF), Memorial Museum Passchendaele 1917 (MMP/VF), Milo-Profi Photography (MPP/VF), Westtoer (W/VF); WBT-JP Remy (WBT-JPR); Wikimedia Commons (WC): Isabelle Bruneel, CC BY-SA 4.0 (IB/WC), Havang(nl), CC0 (H/WC), Mathieu.clabaut, CC BY-SA 3.0 (Mc/WC), Velvet, CC BY-SA 4.0 (V/WC), Wernervc, CC BY-SA 3.0 (W/WC); Wikipedia: Conniption, CC BY-SA 3.0 (C/W)

Front cover Red poppy field, France (TK/A)
Back cover, clockwise from left Ring of Remembrance, Notre-Dame de Lorette French National War Cemetery (T/S), Somme American Cemetery (AI/S), Sanctuary Wood/Hill 62, the Ypres Salient (CG/S)
Title page, clockwise from left Brooding soldier, Vancouver Corner (NA/S), Dodengang trenches near Diksmuide (EA/S), German graves, Saint-Symphorien Cemetery (PD/S)
Part openers Page 1: Horse and cart outside Ypres (MMP/VF); page 13: German zeppelin (MMP/VF); page 45: Battle of Verdun (EC/S)

Maps David McCutcheon FBCart.S. FRGS

Typeset by Ian Spick, Bradt Guides
Production managed by Zenith Media; printed in the UK
Digital conversion by www.dataworks.co.in

Paper used for this product comes from sustainably managed forests, recycled and controlled sources.

Contents

LIST OF MAPS

KEY TO SYMBOLS

————	The Western Front	⚱	Museum
▬▬▬	International border	✝	Church/chapel
– – – –	Départmental boundary	⬒	Cemetery
▦▦▦	Motorway	⬧	Memorial/statue
════	Main road	✳	Viewpoint
═══	Secondary road	ᛞ	Historic railway
———	Other road	○	Crater
▭▭▭	Railway	⬭	Bunker
✈	Airport	⬟	Minefields
🄿	Parking	✕	Battlefield
ⓘ	Tourist information	♧	Notable tree/woodland feature
⊞	Historic/important building	•	Other point of interest
⛫	Tower/fortress	∿∿∿∿	Trenches
⌂	Memorial archway	▨	Urban area

Introduction

When Germany declared war on France on 3 August 1914, what was meant to be a quick war 'over by Christmas' turned into four years of attrition. Both sides dug in and a line of trenches stretching from the North Sea to the Swiss border created a line known as the Western Front. From 1914 to 1918, this line only fluctuated by a few miles in either direction as the Germans fought to reach the North Sea (to cut off Allied supply routes) and the Allies (the British, French, Canadians, Americans Australians and New Zealanders (ANZAC Forces), and the South Africans) attempted to push them back. By the end of World War I, total human casualties numbered over 37 million – of which over 16 million died and 20 million were wounded. It ranks as the sixth-deadliest conflict in human history.

From 2014 to 2018, World War I centenary celebrations and remembrances took place across the world, but nowhere with more verve than France and Belgium where the battles were played out. This practical guide covers all the main cemeteries, memorials and museums in these countries, as well as practical information on how to reach them, how to research a lost family member and the best guided tours. It is tailored specifically for visitors, both young and old, planning pilgrimages to visit relatives that fought in the war or for those just wanting to learn more about this dark period of history – 'Lest we forget'.

Acknowledgements

Thanks and gratitude to our Bradt project manager Claire Strange, cartographer David McCutcheon, contributor Doug Goodman, and the following regional experts for their assistance: Benoît Diéval, Anita Rampall, Peter Francis, Sophie Wicke, Nele Rubrecht, Nathalie Vanraepenbusch, Michelle Martens, Christelle Clement, Lea Manot and Juliette Delcourt.

DEDICATION

Dedicated to Herbert John Ruler, who died in France aged 18, and to all who perished in the Great War

HOW TO USE THIS GUIDE

ACCESSIBILITY Where sites and museums are wheelchair accessible, we have indicated this by including ♿ in the practical information.

FEEDBACK REQUEST AND UPDATES WEBSITE

At Bradt Guides we're aware that guidebooks start to go out of date on the day they're published – and that you, our readers, are out there in the field doing research of your own. You'll find out before us when a fine new family-run hotel opens or a favourite restaurant changes hands and goes downhill. So why not tell us about your experiences? Contact us on ☎ 01753 893444 or e info@bradtguides.com. We will forward emails to the author who may post updates on the Bradt website at w bradtguides.com/updates. Alternatively, you can add a review of the book to Amazon, or share your adventures with us on social media:

f BradtGuides
X BradtGuides & @emmasthomson
☉ BradtGuides & @emmathomsontravels

Part One

GENERAL INFORMATION

Background Information

WORLD WAR I TIMELINE

1914

28 June–27 July The assassination of Archduke Franz Ferdinand by a Bosnian Serb assassin, Gavrilo Princip, in Sarajevo leads to Kaiser Wilhelm II promising Germany's support in the event of retaliation against Serbia.

28 July Austria–Hungary declares war on Serbia and British fleets are ordered to war bases.

3 August Germany declares war on France and invades Belgium and Luxembourg.

4 August At 23.00 Britain declares war on Germany.

23 August The first major battle begins (and ends) at Mons in Belgium with the British forced to retreat in the face of greater German manpower and artillery (see box, page 41).

9 September Allied forces halt the German advance into France during the First Battle of the Marne.

22 September–end of November The first battles of Picardy, Albert, Arras and Ypres take place.

26 & 29 October Nieuwpoort sluice gates are opened to flood the plain and halt the German advance (see box, page 40).

German infantry on the battlefield in the opening days of World War I (WC)

1915

25 September Start of the Battle of Loos (see box, page 70). British soldiers, forced to pull off inefficient masks, choke on their own gas as it blows back across the lines. Battle ends on 6 October.

1916

21 February A huge loss by the French at the Battle of Verdun (see box, page 107), the longest of the war, leads the British to start the Battle of the Somme as a diversionary tactic.
1 July Battle of the Somme begins (see box, page 80). Over a period of 4½ months the British Army, despite capturing key positions, advances only a few miles before winter sets in and fighting ceases.

1917

16 April 1917 Nivelle Offensive at the Chemin des Dames, which should have been '*La der des ders*' ('The last battle').
7–14 June Battle of Messines – regarded as one of Britain's greatest war victories (see box, page 34).
31 July The final phase of the Third Battle of Ypres in Belgium grinds on into the autumn and winter (see box, page 25).
20 November The Battle of Cambrai sees 450 tanks pitted against the German Front Line.

1918

15 July Second Battle of the Marne in Champagne shows signs of German collapse.
8 August Allies' advance is successful.
4 October Germany seeks an armistice.
9 November Kaiser abdicates.
11 November Armistice is signed in a railway carriage in the Oise region on the 11th hour of the 11th day of the 11th month. World War I ends.

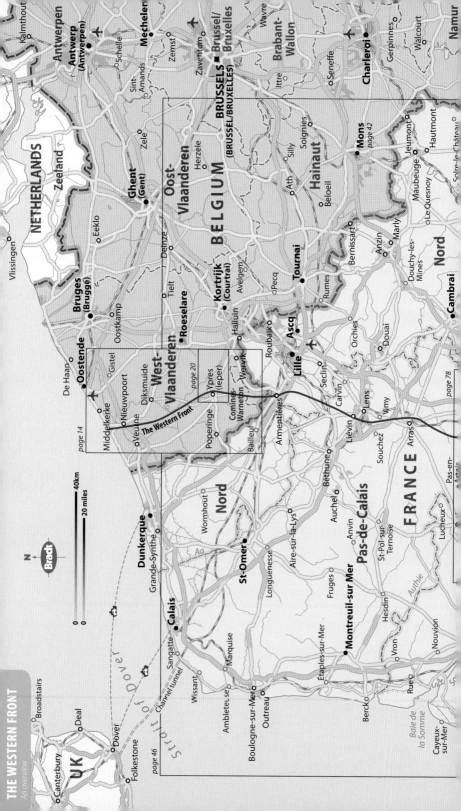

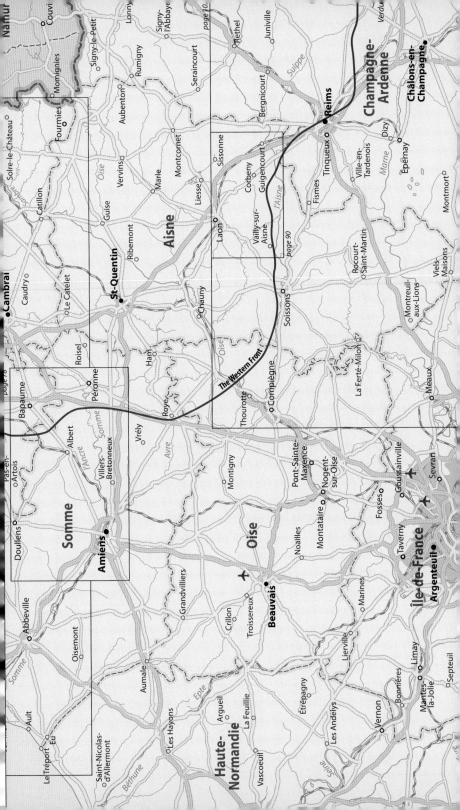

2

Practical Information

GETTING THERE AND AWAY

BY AIR Brussels Airlines (w *brusselsairlines.com*) and British Airways (w *ba.com*) fly direct to Brussels from most major UK cities.

BY FERRY The faster Eurostar and Eurotunnel services have heavily eclipsed travel by boat, but for families it remains the cheapest option. **P&O Ferries** (\ *01304 448888;* w *poferries.com*) and **DFDS Seaways** (\ *0871 574 7235;* w *dfds.com*) both operate a Dover–Calais route. For Belgian battlefields, DFDS Seaways also have a daily Dover–Dunkerque service; P&O Ferries likewise operate a daily overnight service to Zeebrugge.

BY TRAIN
From the UK
Eurostar (\ *03432 186186;* w *eurostar.com*) runs up to nine services a day from London St Pancras to Lille, Paris or Brussels via the Channel Tunnel. Advance booking essential; the earlier you book the greater chance of a cheap fare. If you're travelling to Belgium be sure to select the 'Any Belgian Station' option from the 'Belgium' drop-down menu when booking online, as this allows you to travel on to Ypres or Poperinge, for example, for free. The fastest London–Brussels journey time is 2 hours.

Le Shuttle (Eurotunnel; \ *03443 353535;* w *eurotunnel.com*) is a high-speed car train that runs from Folkestone to Calais in 35 minutes. Book early and travel outside peak times for the best rates.

From France, Germany, Luxembourg and the Netherlands
Thalys (\ *0032 (0)70 66 77 88;* w *thalys.com*) provides an inter-Europe network with connections between all major western European cities.

BY COACH At the time of writing, **National Express** (w *nationalexpress.com*) have paused their bus routes to Europe, but should revive them at the end of 2023. Check their website for updates. **Blablacar** (w *blablacar.com*) offer London to Lille or Brussels routes departing from Victoria Station. Finally, **Megabus** (\ *0900 160 0900;* w *uk.megabus.com*) operate from a host of UK cities to Brussels, Lille and Amiens (for the Somme).

GETTING AROUND

BY CAR Many of the World War I battlefields, memorials and cemeteries are located in the countryside so it really helps to have your own car. Remember to drive on the right, take sufficient cash to pay at French motorway tollbooths

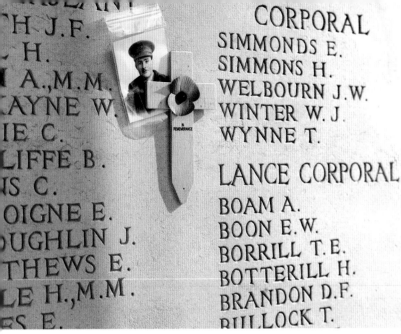

CORPORAL

SIMMONDS E.
SIMMONS H.
WELBOURN J.W.
WINTER W.J.
WYNNE T.

LANCE CORPORAL

BOAM A.
BOON E.W.
BORRILL T.E.
BOTTERILL H.
BRANDON D.F.
BULLOCK T.

Putting a face to the fallen is now increasingly possible (MPP/VF)

(*péages*) and observe *priorité à droite* (give way to the right on secondary roads and roundabouts). In Belgium, it's illegal to drive without carrying headlamp adapters, a warning triangle, reflective vest, first-aid kit and fire extinguisher in your car, so be prepared.

BY TRAIN

In France *with thanks to French rail travel expert Peter Mills.*
There is an extensive network of local trains serving towns both large and small, and the French national rail network, **SNCF** (w *uk.voyages-sncf.com*), operates a number of different types of services. **TGV** (*Train à Grande Vitesse*; w *tgv.com/en*) is a high-speed, long-distance service (booking prior to travel is essential), and **OUIGO** (w *uk.voyages-sncf.com/en/ouigo-low-cost-train*) is SNCF's new high-speed, low-fare service. **TER** (*Transport Express Régional*; w *ter-sncf.com*) is a network of regional trains – there's no need to book in advance; simply buy a ticket at the station. Timetable leaflets (*fiches horaires*) are available in all stations. **Intercités** (w *intercites.sncf.com*) is a classic French rail service with medium- and long-distance services. Bikes are allowed on most trains, but check individual websites for details.

In Belgium The national rail network is run by **SNCB-NMBS** (♦ *02 70 79 79 79*; w *belgiantrain.be*). Tickets can be bought online, at the station or on board as a last resort. Folding bicycles are allowed on trains free of charge; anything else costs €4 supplement on top of your train ticket.

BY BIKE Numerous local tourist offices rent bikes and have specially tailored World War I bike trail maps for sale. These have been listed under individual towns. Worth approaching first are the tourist offices in Pas de Calais (page 61), Somme (page 79) and Aisne (page 91), who are happy to supply a First World War Heritage brochure with biking trails, on request. Also see box on page 18.

2

'The Last Post' is sounded at the Menin Gate (MPP/VF)

TOURIST INFORMATION

There are no tourist offices for Flanders as yet in Australia, Ireland and New Zealand.

FRANCE

Australia French Tourist Bureau, 25 Bligh St – level 22, Sydney, NSW 2000; ☏ + 61 29210 5400

Belgium/Luxembourg Av Louise, 222 1050 Brussels; ☏ + 322 505 38 28

Canada 1800 Av McGill Collège, Suite 490, Montreal, Québec H3A 3J6; ☏ +1 514 288 2026

Germany French Embassy, Zeppelinallee 37, D-60325 Frankfurt am Main; ☏ +49 499 758 0148

The Netherlands Prinsengracht 670 1017 KX, Amsterdam; ☏ +31 20 535 30 10

South Africa c/o Air France Village Walk Office, Tower Bldg, 3rd floor, cnr of Maud & Rivonia Rd, Sandton; ☏ +27 11 523 8252

UK (London office) Lincoln Hse, 300 High Holborn, London WC1V 7JH; ☏ 020 7061 6600 (60p/min); ⏱ 10.00–16.00 Mon–Fri; e info.uk@france.fr; w uk.france.fr; click on Nord-Pas de Calais; information includes links to regional & local websites.

See also separate sites for more details on each region of Hauts de France, Marne, Champagne & Verdun.

USA 825 Third Av, New York, NY 10022; ☏ +1 212 838 7800; also 9454 Wilshire Bd – Suite 210, Beverley Hills, Los Angeles, CA 90212; ☏ +1 310 271 2693 & 205 N Michigan Av – Suite 3770, Chicago IL 6060; ☏ +1 312 327 0290

BELGIUM

Belgium Visit Flanders: Rue du Marché aux Herbes 61, Brussels; ☏ +322 504 03 90; w toerismevlaanderen.be; Visit Brussels: Rue Royale 2, Brussels; ☏ +322 513 89 70; w visitbrussels.be

UK & Australia 1a Cavendish Sq, London W1G 0LD; ☏ +44 020 7307 7738; w visitflanders.com

USA & Canada The New York Times Bldg, 620 8th Av, 44th Flr, New York; ☏ +1 212 584 2336 3002; w visitflanders.com

BATTLEFIELD TOURS

Battlefield tours are largely operated by ex-soldiers, military historians and other experts whose initial interest stemmed from tracing their own missing relatives. Many offer small bespoke tours by minibus but cycling and walking tours are also available.

Online records of many missing relatives can now be downloaded for free, or for a small fee or by subscription. Start with the free and simple-to-use **CWGC** app (w *cwgc.org/who-we-are/our-apps*), available for Android and iOS phones, which allows you to search for war graves at more than 23,000 locations in more than 150 countries and territories.

If you'd prefer human help, the **Commonwealth War Graves Commission** (*2 Marlow Rd, Maidenhead, Berks, SL6 7DX;* 01628 634221; e *enquiries@cwgc. org;* w *cwgc.org*) hold records for 1.9 million Commonwealth men and women – with more bodies still being unearthed. They also have an office in Ypres (Ieper), Belgium (page 15). The **Verdun Memorial Museum** also has a documentation centre (page 108) open to all by appointment.

Before starting, arm yourself with as much information as possible. Photographs, medals, diaries or letters can provide a rough idea of which armed force your relative served in, be it land, sea or air. Other likely sources include general or regimental museums such as the **Imperial War Museums** (w *iwm.org*) and **Royal Artillery Museum** (w *royalartillerymuseum.com*), libraries and national archive collections, along with newspaper and photographic libraries. Census records, town archives, village memorials and memorials in churches may also help point you in the right direction. So, too, can social media.

Also try the **Royal, Indian & Dominion Navy Casualties** (w *navel-history.net*), **Royal Navy and Royal Marines War Graves Roll 1914–1919** (w *nationalarchives.gov.uk*) and **Ancestry** (w *ancestry.co.uk*).

Finally, the **RAF Museum Hendon** (w *rafmuseum.org.uk*) in North London holds casualty cards giving details of the aircraft involved and sometimes details of the next of kin.

Tour organisers catering for students or school children will find **The Great War 1914–1918** (w *greatwar.co.uk*) section 'WW1 Education Resources for Teachers' especially useful.

Advance Battlefield Tours 01423 408077; w advancebattlefieldtours.co.uk. Small tailor-made tours taking in main tourist areas, with advice on tracing relatives.

Anglia Tours 01376 574130; w angliatours. co.uk. Coach tours for schools & special-interest groups from churches & sports clubs to parents' associations.

Back-Roads Touring Co Battlefield Tours 020 8987 0990; w backroadstouring.co.uk. Include battlefield visits as part of a wider programme using 16-seater mini coaches.

Battle Honours 01438 989129; w battle-honours.co.uk. Concentrate on off-the-beaten-track walking tours for groups up to 16. Director & joint owner Clive Harris served in the Royal Signals. Canadian office too.

Bird Battlefield Tours 020 8752 0956/01243 789077; w birdbattlefieldtours.com. Tours encourage dinner-table discussions for groups of 4–16, inclusive of ferry or flights.

The Cultural Experience 0345 475 1815; w theculturalexperience.com. Offers coach & other bespoke tours for 6–20 people on a variety of topics.

Dr Thomson's Tours 01227 455922; w drttours.co.uk. Tours, led by Dr Andrew Thomson, who has a PhD in history, take up to 5 people in AC Citroën C8 minivan or rental vehicles.

Eyewitness Tours 01306 880960; w eyewitnesstours.com. Led by former history teacher Andy Thompson who has been studying war & conflict for 40 years. Tours home in on the lives of individual soldiers.

Practical Information   BATTLEFIELD TOURS

2

AFRICAN SOLDIERS Soldiers from Nigeria, the Gold Coast, Sierra Leone, The Gambia and other African colonies patriotically enlisted in their droves during World War I, but it was not until 1915, and faced with a staggering loss of lives, that Lord Kitchener – the Secretary of State for War – allowed black fighters from Britain, the Caribbean and Africa to take part in European frontline combat.

Until then – fearful that black servicemen fighting a white enemy were a possible threat to imperialism – their role had been limited to menial tasks such as digging trenches and moving artillery shells. Yet many had travelled at their own expense to join the Allied forces and, unfairly, it is only relatively recently that their stories of courage have come to light.

Shockingly, during the Victory Parade in London on 19 July 1919, thousands of British, French, American, Belgian and Greek troops marched past the newly created cenotaph to pay their respects to fallen comrades, but no black units were invited to take part. It was less than a year since the war had ended and already black soldiers were being deliberately forgotten.

BRITISH WEST INDIES REGIMENT (BWIR) In 1915, the British West Indies Regiment (BWIR) was formed as a separate black unit within the British Army. The first recruits sailed from Jamaica to Britain and arrived in October 1915 to train at a camp near Seaford on the Sussex coast. Mostly led by white officers, the 3rd and 4th battalions were sent to France and Belgium in July 1916 as non-combatant soldiers to work as ammunition carriers. By the war's end, a total of 15,204 recruits had served in the BWIR, with a loss of 185 soldiers (killed or died of wounds). A further 1,071 died of illness and 697 were wounded. In Seaford Cemetery there are more than 300 Commonwealth War Graves, of which 19 are of BWIR soldiers.

SOUTH AFRICAN NATIVE LABOUR CORPS (SANLC) While white South Africans fought in their thousands, black South Africans were confined to labour battalions; in particular, the South African Native Labour Corps (SANLC), who were completely segregated from other Allied soldiers. They were not allowed out of the camps without an escort, nor were they allowed in shops or bars or to be entertained in the homes of Europeans. Lieutenant Colonel Godley, second in command of the unit, likened their housing to that of German prisoners of war. No medals were awarded even though the British government had provided one for all who had served with the SANLC.

Among the very few references in Britain are the names on Hollybrook Memorial, Southampton, of those who died when the troop carrier ship SS *Mendi* sank in 1917. Again, no medals were awarded, despite medals being presented to black members from the neighbouring British Protectorates of Basutoland (modern Lesotho), Bechuanaland (Botswana) and Swaziland (Eswatini).

BLACK AMERICANS For black Americans, descended from enslaved Africans, the entry of the United States into the war in 1917 provided an ideal chance to prove their patriotism in hopes of being recognised as full citizens. More than 20,000 initially enlisted for military service and by July 1917 this had increased to 700,000. While they were barred from joining the Marines and only allowed to serve menial roles in the Navy, they were able to serve in all branches of the Army except for the aviation units, and the first battalions arrived in France in 1917.

Perhaps the most famous of these was the 369th United States Infantry, a regiment of African American combat troops, who quickly earned the nickname the Harlem Hell Fighters because of their fighting prowess. They also provided the longest service of any regiment in a foreign army, fighting in the trenches for 191 days. The entire regiment received the French Croix de Guerre medal for their actions at Maison-en-Champagne.

INDIAN SOLDIERS India provided the largest force assembled in history during World War I. Around 1.4 million Muslim, Sikh and Hindu men from Indian regions such as the Punjab, Uttar Pradesh, Maharashtra, Tamil Nadu and Bihar volunteered for the Indian Expeditionary Force. Enlisting offered them a chance to break through the caste system to become part of the high-status 'warrior' caste. It also paid well.

It was Indian *jawans* (junior soldiers) who stopped the German advance at Ypres in the autumn of 1914 while the British were still recruiting and training their own forces, and hundreds were killed in a gallant but futile engagement at Neuve Chappelle on 10–13 March 1915.

Overall, around 74,000 died, 67,000 were wounded and 10,000 were reported missing, while 98 Indian army nurses were killed. Those with no known grave are commemorated on the Menin Gate in Ypres (Ieper), Belgium and at Neuve Chapelle in France.

A LEGACY REMEMBERED The Black Poppy Rose (w *blackpoppyrose.org*), launched in September 2010 by cultural and ancestral genealogist Selena Carty, symbolises honourable contributions made by African, West Indian, Caribbean, Pacific Island and other black or indigenous communities to global wars since the 16th century, with the hope that future generations will be inspired by these largely untold historical legacies.

The Harlem Hell Fighters (EC/S)

In Flanders Fields…the Dodengang trenches near Diksmuide, Belgium (MPP/VF)

Flanders By Bike w flandersbybike.com. Cycling company that offers a 100km 14–18 Western Front Route.

Great Rail Journeys 01904 734154; w greatrail.com. Selection of rail/cruise battlefield tours offered as part of general coverage of France & Belgium.

Holts Tours Battlefields and History 01709 385500; w holts.co.uk. Founded by Tonie & Valmai Holt back in 1975, this company specialising in educational travel is now part of Leger Shearings Group.

In the Footsteps 01989 565599; w inthefootsteps.com. Tailor-made tours by experts in a variety of topics.

Leger Holidays Guided Battlefield Coach Tours 01709 385624; w legerbattlefields.co.uk. Offers 20 World War I battlefield tours.

Martin Randall Travel 020 8742 3355; w martinrandall.com. Selection of World War I-related topics as part of their respected history & battle tours.

On The Go Tours 020 7371 1113; w onthegotours.com. Offers 2 4-day tours, focusing on ANZAC sites, travelling via coach or Eurostar.

Rifleman Tours 01908 617264; w riflemantours.co.uk. Run by husband-&-wife team Tony & Allison Eden, who offer tours for 12–18 people, from the first-time battlefield visitor to the serious researcher.

Shearings 0344 824 6351; w shearings.com. Selection of battlefields among their specialist coach tours.

Trafalgar 0800 533 5619; w trafalgar.com. Coach tours to major World War I sites.

APPS

WESTERN FRONT WAY There's a pay-for app offering story-led trails along World War I Front Line routes that can be hiked or biked using detailed maps at w thewesternfrontway.com. Available from the Apple Store or Google Play.

NGĀ TAPUWAE TRAILS A free app and audio guide (w *ngatapuwae.govt.nz*), which you can also print off as an e-book, has been developed offering a series of nine trails (five in Belgium, four in France) that guide visitors around all the battlefield and memorial sites associated with New Zealand soldiers around Ypres, Belgium and Arras, France. The multimedia content and maps are very good. Download from the Apple App Store or Google Play for Android.

Part Two

BELGIUM

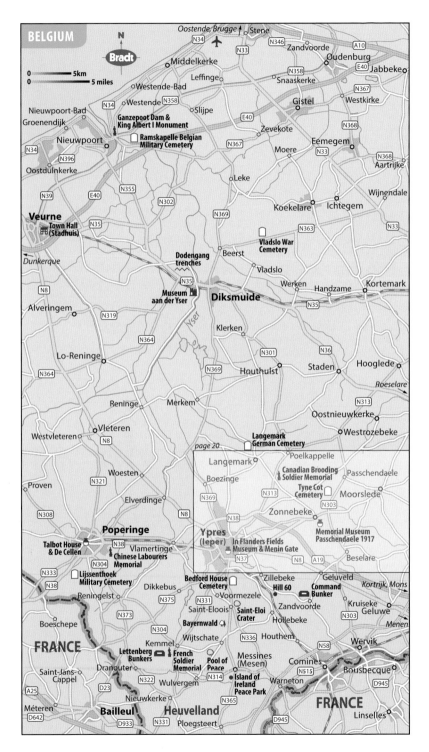

N

Bradt

0 ————— 5km
0 ————— 5 miles

Oostende, Brugge N34 ✈ Stene
N33
N346 Zandvoorde A10
Oudenburg E40 Jabbeke
Middelkerke
Leffinge N358 Snaaskerke
Westende-Bad Gistel N367 Westkirke
Westende N358
Slijpe E40 Zevekote N368
Nieuwpoort-Bad N34
Groenendijk Ganzepoot Dam & Eemegem
King Albert I Monument Moere N33
Nieuwpoort Ramskapelle Belgian N367
N34 Military Cemetery N368
N396 Aartrijke
Oostdulnkerke Leke Wijnendale
N39 E40 N355
N302 Koekelare Ichtegem
Veurne N369
Town Hall N35 N363 N33
(Stadhuis) Vladslo War
Cemetery
Dodengang Beerst
Dunkerque trenches Vladslo
N35 Werken Handzame Kortemark
Museum Diksmuide N35
aan der Yser
Alveringem N319 Klerken
N364 N301 N36
Lo-Reninge N369 Staden Hooglede
N364 Houthulst
Roeselare
Reninge Merkem
N313
Westvleteren Vleteren Oostnieuwkerke
N8 Langemark Westrozebeke
page 20 German Cemetery
Langemark Poelkappelle
Woesten Boezinge Canadian Brooding Passchendaele
Proven N321 Soldier Memorial
N369 Tyne Cot Moorslede
Elverdinge N313 Cemetery N303
N308 N8 Zonnebeke
Poperinge N38 Ypres Memorial Museum
Talbot House N38 (Ieper) Passchendaele 1917
& De Cellen Vlamertinge In Flanders Fields
N304 Chinese Labourers Museum & Menin Gate
N333 Memorial N37 N8 A19 Beselare
N38 Lijssenthoek Zillebeke Geluveld
Military Cemetery Dikkebus Bedford House Kortrijk, Mons
Reningelst N375 Cemetery Hill 60 Command
N331 Voormezele Bunker Kruiseke Geluwe
N373 Saint-Eloois Zandvoorde N303
Boeschepe N304 Saint-Eloi Menen
Bayernwald Crater Hollebeke
FRANCE Kemmel Wijtschate N336 Houthem Wervik
Lettenberg French N58
Saint-Jans- Bunkers Soldier Pool of Messines Comines
Cappel Dranouter Memorial Peace (Mesen) N515 Bousbecque
A25 D23 N322 Wulvergem N314 Island of Warneton D945
Nieuwkerke Ireland
Méteren Peace Park FRANCE
D642 Bailleul Heuvelland N365 Linselles
D933 N331 Ploegsteert D945

3

Ypres and the Ypres Salient

YPRES (IEPER)

Ypres – or 'Wipers' as it was nicknamed by British soldiers – is a relatively small town with a very famous history. War arrived here on 7 October 1914 when 10,000 German troops entered the town, kidnapped the burgomaster, stole 62,000 francs from the city coffers and demanded the local bakers prepare 8,000 loaves of bread to feed the soldiers. The next morning they released the burgomaster and marched west towards Vlamertinghe. The Germans never entered the city again and residents felt safe enough to stay put until May 1915 when chlorine gas was deployed on the battlefields. As the war progressed, Ypres became a strategic defence point of the Ypres Salient (page 19) and was battered by artillery fire. When locals returned at the end of the war, it was barely recognisable. It's said you could sit on horseback and look over the town without a single building interrupting your view.

GETTING THERE AND AWAY

By car If travelling from Calais or Dunkerque, leave the E40 at exit 1a and follow the N8 south to Ypres (*53km; approx 50mins*). Remember, Ypres is known as 'Ieper' in Flanders and can change on road signs. From Lille, follow the A25/E42 west and then join the N58 leading north past Armentières; after a few miles turn left on to the N336 towards Ypres (*40km; approx 40mins*).

By train Brussels-Zuid/Bruxelles-Midi (*41mins past the hour Mon–Fri, 36mins past the hour Sat–Sun; 1hr 45mins*); Brugge via Kortrijk (*32mins past the hour daily; 1hr 49mins*); Gent via Kortrijk (*9mins past the hour daily; 1hr 12mins*). Trains from Lille to Ypres require about four changes; for times, consult w eurail.com and w belgiantrain.be.

TOURIST INFORMATION

Ypres Tourist Office Lakenhalle, 34 Grote Markt; 057 23 92 20; w toerismeieper.be; 1 Apr–15 Nov 09.00–18.00 Mon–Fri, 10.00–18.00 Sat–Sun; 16 Nov–30 Mar 09.00–17.00 Mon–Fri, 10.00–17.00 Sat–Sun. A large well-equipped office that can organise hotel bookings & battlefield tours, & sells self-guided tour maps (see box, page 18).

Commonwealth War Graves Commission (CWGC) Menenstraat 33; w cwgc.org; 13.00–21.00 Tue, Thu, Fri & Sun, 10.00–21.00 Wed & Sat. Has an office near the Menin Gate that can assist with finding a grave or place of commemoration in the British & Commonwealth military cemeteries. No appointment needed. They also have an app. Wreaths can also be purchased if you wish to lay one by a family member's grave.

In Flanders Fields Museum, Ypres (MPP/VF)

GUIDED TOURS

2Xplore Flanders Fields ☎0475 51 98 28; e info@2xplore.be; w 2xplore.be. Run by English-speaking guide Patrick who served in the Belgian Armed Forces for 20 years in active war zones, thus lending a unique perspective. Offers standard or custom tours from 5–8hrs (€50–80), as well as evening tours from 18.00 for €35pp.

Camalou Guided Battlefield Tours ☎057 20 43 42; e info@visit-ypres.be; w camalou.com. 2-man team who offer a very thorough 3-day/2-night itinerary tailored to British, USA, New Zealand, Australian & Canadian travellers from €860pp.

Flanders Battlefield Tours ☎057 36 04 60; e info@ypres-fbt.com; w ypres-fbt.com. Englishwoman Genevra Charsley & her Flemish husband study & conduct research all winter, so come summertime their tours are the city's best. Very knowledgeable, friendly & accommodating. Their 2½hr Short Tour visits Hill 60, Polygon Wood & the Hooge Crater trenches & costs €30pp. The larger 4hr North & South Salient tours cost €38pp.

THE WIPERS TIMES

In 1916, the 12th Battalion Sherwood Foresters from Nottingham and Derbyshire Regiment stumbled across an abandoned printing press while stationed in Ypres. One of their men was able to salvage it and they printed off a trial paper, calling it *The Wipers Times* after the British nickname for Ypres. Filled with poems and hugely satirical, it included entries such as:

WEATHER FORECAST:

5 to 1	Mist
11 to 2	East Wind or Frost
8 to 1	Chlorine

(ET)

The trench magazine became hugely popular and, in 2013, the BBC broadcast a dramatisation about its creation, and a new theatre production created by Ian Hislop hit the West End in London in 2017. The Browerij de Kazematten in Ypres produces a delicious 6.2% abv pale ale in their honour – look for it in local cafés.

Their silver minibuses depart from the public bus stop on Grote Markt.

Great War Pilgrimage Tours 0476 22 96 36; e sabinedeclercq72@hotmail.com; w greatwarpilgrimage.com. Born & raised near Ypres, Sabine offers bespoke battlefield tours. Prices on request.

Salient Tours British Grenadier Bookshop, 5 Meensestraat; 057 21 46 57; e tours@ salienttours.be; w salienttours.be. Provide a range of morning, afternoon & longer tours – email for the latest offerings.

Cycling the Western Front 0475 81 06 08; e carl.ooghe@gmail.com; w cyclingthewesternfront.co.uk. Offers tours through Flanders Fields, the Somme, Arras & Vimy Ridge, either on a commuter bike (35–50km) or a road bike (75–100km).

WHAT TO SEE AND DO

In Flanders Fields Museum (*Grote Markt 34; 057 23 92 20; w inflandersfields. be; 1 Apr–30 Sep 10.00–18.00 Mon–Fri, 10.00–17.00 Sat & Sun; 1 Oct–31 Mar 10.00–17.00 Tue–Sun; adult/19–25/7–18/under 7s €10/6/5/free; audio guide €2; with help*) Located on the second floor of the Lakenhalle, this high-tech museum centres around the 'poppy bracelet'. It's issued to you on arrival and then you input your name and place of birth and the computer selects personal stories of people from your town or county who participated in the war. You'll then be able to print or email the stories to your smartphone and create an itinerary to visit the areas where they fought. You can keep the bracelet as a souvenir and forgo the €1 deposit. Entry to the bell tower costs an extra €2, but is well worth it for the views overlooking famous battlegrounds. Be aware that it's a steep climb and not accessible to wheelchair users. It also has a **knowledge centre** (*057 23 94 50; mornings by appointment only & then 13.00–17.00 Mon, Tue, Thu & Fri, 10.00– 12.00 & 13.00–17.00 Wed*), which individuals can use to trace relatives.

Saint George's Memorial Church (*Elverdingsestraat 1; 057 21 56 86; w stgeorgesmemorialchurchypres.com; 10.00–17.00 daily; free entry*) This unassuming church was designed by Sir Reginald Bloomfield – the architect responsible for the Menin Gate – in 1929. It's filled with brass plaques honouring fallen soldiers and furniture donated by the victims' families. The stained-glass windows dedicated to various individuals and regiments are moving too, especially

Saint George's Memorial Church, Ypres (P/S)

Visiting sites where family members may have died in battle is emotional and for many a pilgrimage of sorts. If you'd prefer privacy, why not rent a bike and take off on your own? The tourist board sells two maps. The 28.5km *Mine Warfare: Messines Ridge 1917* and 35km *Ypres Salient* route (€3) uses Flanders' regional numbered cycling network. The accompanying booklet comes in English and has useful aerial photographs, diagrams and explanations of the various sites. Or, if you're feeling a bit more confident, the unsignposted circular 45km *Vredes* route (€2) departs from the Grote Markt and, among others, takes in Essex Farm Cemetery, Langemark, the Vancouver Corner, Tyne Cot and Hill 62. Explanations are in Dutch only.

If you don't fancy all that pedalling, take the car and follow the 82km *In Flanders Fields* route (€3), which takes in Poperinge, Messines and Zonnebeke, or the 70km *Ypres Salient* route.

the window on the right above the baptistry which remembers Captain Boyce Combe. He was killed on 11 November 1914 at the tender age of 26 and, although he has no known grave, his name appears on the Menin Gate.

Menin Gate (Meninpoort) (*Meensestraat;* w *lastpost.be*) Erected in July 1927, the Menin Gate marks the spot where soldiers would leave town on their way to the Front Line. Carved into the interior walls are the names of 54,896 British and

Menin Gate, Ypres (NA/S)

Commonwealth soldiers killed in World War I and whose graves are unknown. Soldiers who went missing after 16 August 1917 have their names inscribed on the arches at Tyne Cot Cemetery (page 27). As a mark of respect, the road is closed every evening at 20.00 and members of the local fire brigade sound their bugles. The former chief bugler, Antoine Verschoot – who sadly passed away in 2015 – sounded his horn for over 61 years. Known as the 'Last Post', this tribute to the fallen has continued uninterrupted since 2 July 1928, except under German occupation during World War II when the ceremony was conducted in Brookwood Military Cemetery in Surrey. A verse from Laurence Binyon's poem *For the Fallen* is usually read aloud too. It's best to start queueing around 19.30 to get a good view. On 17 April 2023, restoration work began on the gate – scaffolding the exterior and all inscribed panels – and is due to last two years, with an expected completion date of March 2025. The panels can be viewed as part of a computer-generated fly-through inside the CWGC Ieper Information Centre (page 15) and visitors can instead see the eight artworks entitled *Menin Gate Moments*, by renowned *War Horse* illustrator Tom Clohosy Cole, displayed on the ramparts of the memorial gate. The Last Post ceremonies will continue every night on the bridge in front of the gate.

Indian Forces Memorial Positioned behind the Menin Gate, this memorial featuring four lions is dedicated to the 130,000 soldiers of the Indian Forces who served in Flanders during World War I.

THE YPRES SALIENT

A salient is a military defence line that bulges into enemy territory and is surrounded on three sides. The one which developed around the town of Ypres (Ieper) during World War I was a result of the failure of the German Schlieffen Plan. Their aim was to avoid fighting a war on two fronts by invading France, then capturing its sea ports and Paris, via Belgium, before Russian troops could mobilise on the east German border. The attack relied on speed and the element of surprise. The Germans lost both when they were caught unawares by the Belgian Resistance who delayed German troops for over a month until French and British soldiers arrived. Both sides dug in: the Allies (British, French, Canadians and Belgians) defending the coastline and the Germans pushing towards it. Both sides built trenches in the soil that stretched for 400 miles from Nieuwpoort to the French/Swiss border, a line known as the Western Front. The contours of

IN FLANDERS FIELDS

Lieutenant Colonel John McCrae, published 8 December 1915

In Flanders fields the poppies blow,
Between the crosses, row on row,
That mark our place; and in the sky,
The larks, still bravely singing, fly
Scarce heard amid the guns below.

We are the Dead. Short days ago
We lived, felt dawn, saw sunset glow.
Loved, and were loved, and now we lie
In Flanders fields.

Take up our quarrel with the foe:
To you from failing hands we throw
The torch; be yours to hold it high.
If ye break faith with us who die
We shall not sleep, though poppies grow
In Flanders fields.

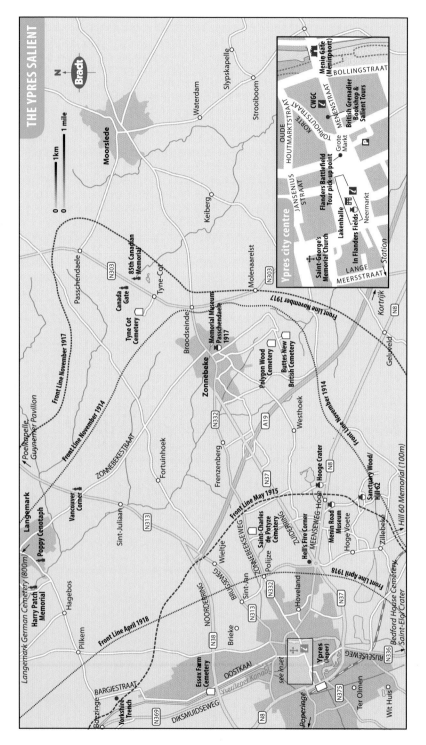

THE YPRES SALIENT

Bradt

N

0 ——— 1km
0 ——— 1 mile

Moorslede

Waterdam

Slypskapelle

Strooiboom

Keiberg

Molenaarelst

Passchendaele

N303

85th Canadian Memorial

Tyne-Cot

Canada Gate

Tyne Cot Cemetery

Memorial Museum Passchendaele 1917

Zonnebeke

Broodseinde

Polygon Wood Cemetery

Buttes New British Cemetery

Front Line November 1917

Kortrijk

N8

Geluveld

Front Line November 1917

Poelkapelle, Guynemer Pavilion

Front Line November 1914

ZONNEBEEKSTRAAT

Fortuinhoek

N332

A19

Westhoek

Front Line November 1914

Langemark
Poppy Cenotaph

Vancouver Corner

Sint-Juliaan

N313

Wieltje

Front Line May 1915

ZONNEBEEKSEWEG

Saint-Charles de Potyze Cemetery

ZUIDERRING

Hooge Crater

Hooge

MEENSEWEG

Menin Road Museum

Hell's Fire Corner

Sanctuary Wood/Hill 62

Hoge Voete

Zillebeke

Hill 60 Memorial (100m)

N8

Langemark German Cemetery (800m)

Harry Patch Memorial

Hagebos

Frenzenberg

NOORDERING

Sint-Jan

N332

Hoveland

N37

Front Line April 1918

Bedford House Cemetery

Saint-Elgi Crater

Pilkem

BRIELENSEWEG

Polijze

N313

Brieke

Front Line April 1918

N38

Essex Farm Cemetery

Ypres (Ieper)

see inset

OOSTKAAI

RIJSELSEWEG

N336

Ter Olmen

Wit Huis

BARGIESTRAAT

Yser/Ieper Kanaal

Yorkshire Trench

Boezinge

N369

DIKSMUIDSEWEG

N8

Poperinge

N375

Ypres city centre

Menin Gate (Meninpoort)

BOLLINGSTRAAT

CWGC

MENENSTRAAT

British Grenadier Bookshop & Salient Tours

KORTE TORHOUTSTRAAT

OUDE HOUTMARKTSTRAAT

Grote Markt

Flanders Battlefield Tour pick-up point

JANSENIUS STRAAT

Lakenhalle

In Flanders Fields

Neermarkt

Saint-George's Memorial Church

LANGE MEERSSTRAAT

Station

this line were established during the First Battle of Ypres when Allied forces fought the Germans for control of Ypres and won, securing the last major town that stood between the Germans and the coast.

Over the next four years, this line would barely move. Vicious trench warfare ensued with increasingly bloody (and muddy) battles being fought in a bid to reach ridges, like Tyne Cot and Hill 60, that would provide elevated views of the battlefield and enemy lines. Ever more ruthless tactics were employed to weaken the enemy, including the use of chlorine and mustard gases, and casualties soared, culminating in the Third Battle of Ypres (see box, page 25), which claimed the lives of over half a million soldiers. By the time the Armistice was signed on 11 November 1918, 1.5 billion shells had been fired on the Western Front and an estimated 750,000 soldiers had lost their lives in the salient. The entire area was a wasteland of death, decay and liquid mud – the only sign of life was the flash of red poppies, whose long-dormant seeds had been brought to the surface. Today, the area is green once more and dotted with cemeteries honouring the fallen soldiers.

ESSEX FARM CEMETERY (*N38 & N369 crossroads; daily; free entry; with help*) Two kilometres north of Ypres city centre, the Essex Farm bunker sat 1,800m from the Front Line and was used as an Advance Dressing Station (ADS). It was here on 3 May 1915 that Canadian surgeon Lieutenant Colonel John McCrae penned one of the most notable poems of World War I, 'In Flanders Fields' (see box, page 19) after witnessing the death of his friend Alexis Helmer the day before. Helmer's name appears on panel ten of the Menin Gate. The poem was sent to *The Spectator* magazine in London, but rejected and eventually published by *Punch* on 8 December 1915. You can visit the bunkers where McCrae tended the wounded, and the adjacent cemetery, where you should look for the grave of rifleman Valentine

Essex Farm Cemetery (NA/S)

Joseph Strudwick – he was killed by a shell two months before his 16th birthday. His tale was true of many poor boys that lied about their age for the chance of regular meals, pay and clothes. You'll note that in many of the cemeteries you visit the spacing and orientation of the headstones change. This indicates that the cemetery sat close to, or on, the Front Line and rather than incorrectly marking the resting place of soldiers whose graves had been destroyed by artillery fire, gaps were left.

FRONT LINE MARKERS

Keep an eye out for metal-fence markers ringing tree saplings dotted around the Ypres Salient. Those marked in blue denote Allied lines; those in red mark the German lines.

YORKSHIRE TRENCH (*Bargiestraat, behind industrial estate;* ⏺ *daily; free entry;* ♿) Accidentally discovered by a farmer behind a Boezinge industrial estate in 1992 and partially excavated by The Diggers, a group of amateur archaeologists (see box, opposite), this British trench dates from 1915 and was acquired by the In Flanders Fields Museum (page 17), where you can see an exhibition of the objects they found. A recent renovation has seen the stairwells renewed, information panels replaced and the trench's original route restored.

SAINT-CHARLES DE POTYZE CEMETERY (*Zonnebeekseweg;* ⏺ *daily; free entry;* ♿ *with help*) Situated 3km northeast of Ypres city centre, this cemetery was incredibly close to the Front Line. The remains of 4,200 French soldiers, including the graves of 69 Muslim fighters, are interred here, as well as a further unidentified 600 souls buried in a mass grave.

HILL 60 (*Zwarteleenstraat 40, Zillebeke*) This manmade hillock – no higher than a second-floor window – was formed in the 1860s during the creation of the Ypres–Comines railway. The steam trains had struggled with the slight incline, so locals had flattened the land and dumped the leftover earth in a pile by the side of the tracks. Prior to the war, the grassy bump was known as Lovers' Knoll, popular with courting couples who came here for a cuddle while enjoying the views. But it was these views that made it the source of intense fighting between the Allied and German forces, and by 1915 it was one of the most feared places on the Front Line. Control of the hill passed back and forth

The remains of a German pillbox at Hill 60 (WM/S)

between British and Germans with a series of suicidal attacks and counterattacks. The biggest breakthrough occurred on 7 June 1917, during the Battle of Messines (see box, page 34), when British tunnellers detonated 53,000lb of explosives under German lines – the resulting craters can still be seen today.

To get there troops had to march past **Hell's Fire Corner**, an infamous roundabout on the Menin Road where German artillery reached within one yard of the road. Several soldiers were killed here before even making it to the Front Line.

BEDFORD HOUSE CEMETERY (*2.5km south of Ypres along Rijselseweg, on left-hand side; free entry; ♿*) 'Bedford House' was the name Commonwealth soldiers gave to Château Rosendal, a moated country house set in woodland, that once stood here. It was used as a field station and as brigade headquarters, but eventually both the trees and house were destroyed by shellfire.

SAINT-ELOI CRATER (*Rijselseweg 214, access through a small green gate; ⊕ 1 Apr–15 Nov 12.00–16.00 daily; free entry*) This pretty reed-strewn pond is the largest of the craters created by the mines detonated during the Battle of Messines (see box, page 34). Nearby stands a British bunker.

MENIN ROAD MUSEUM (*Meenseweg 470, inside Café–Feestzaal Canada; ☏ 057 20 11 36; ⊕ 10.00–22.00 Mon & Wed–Sun; adult/under 12s €4/free*) Small privately owned museum displaying original artefacts recovered from exposed trenches and dugouts.

BOEZINGE

Most people have heard of Passchendaele and Messines and the great battles associated with them, but few have heard of Boezinge – a small village north of Ypres on the banks of the Ieperlee Canal. In April 1915, during the Second Battle of Ypres, the German Army was forcing French troops back across Pilkem Ridge. The French dug in just before reaching the canal and held the Allied Line until the British 4th Division relieved them in June. They began advancing across No Man's Land on 6 July 1915. They sustained heavy losses, but were able to push the Allied Line forward until it was less than 100 yards from the Germans. General Sir Herbert Plumer claimed 'the attack...[was] one of the great battles of the campaign'.

When the war ended, the fighting ground was left fallow and forgotten until the late 1990s when a local volunteer group of archaeologists and historians called The Diggers obtained a permit to excavate. After digging barely 3ft they uncovered trenches, dugouts, thousands of artefacts and undetonated bombs (incredibly the Belgian Army still uncover 200 tonnes every year). Most poignantly, in 2002, behind the Boezinge Industrial Estate, they uncovered the remains of 205 British, German and French soldiers believed to have died in a gas attack. They lay hunched on the ground, still holding their guns and wearing their helmets. Sadly, any identifying markers such as dog tags or uniforms had long since rotted away and none could be identified. Their remains were reinterred in the surrounding cemeteries. The land will be built over soon to make way for the expansion of the estate, and if it hadn't been for The Diggers the efforts of the British 4th Division would have remained buried and forgotten.

British trenches at Hill 62 (WM/S)

SANCTUARY WOOD/HILL 62 (*Canadalaan 26, Zillebeke;* \ *057 46 63 73;* w *hill62trenches. be;* ⏰ *10.00–17.00 Tue–Sun, closed 29 Jul–12 Aug; adult/under 14s €8/5*) Superb privately owned museum that doesn't sanitise the war. The land belonged to a farmer, who left the British trench system and shell holes in place when he returned after the war. It's one of the last original trench systems to survive; most have been filled in. The museum rooms are bursting with accumulated rifles, shell casings, helmets and, best of all, stereoscopes containing original 3D war photographs – although be warned: some of them are quite graphic.

HOOGE CRATER MUSEUM (*Meenseweg 467, Zillebeke;* \ *057 46 84 46;* w *hoogecrater. com;* ⏰ *10.00–18.00 Wed–Sat, 10.00–21.00 Sun, closed Jan & 2nd week of Aug; adult/ student/7–18/under 6s €8.50/6/5/free*) This quaint two-room museum, housed in a 1920s chapel, contains the private collection of curator Niek Benoot-Watteyne and his wife Ilse. They've amassed a good collection of clothing (displayed on mannequins), helmets, shells as well as a 1916 ambulance and a Fokker DR1 German warplane. The now-flooded Hooge Crater lies 100m east. It was created by the British during the Second Battle of Ypres when they smuggled 1,700kg of dynamite down specially built tunnels that ran under the

LANDSCAPES – FEEL FLANDERS' FIELDS

From April 2023 to August 2024 (some exhibitions will run until November 2024), Visit Flanders are hosting a theme year entitled 'Landscapes – Feel Flanders' Fields' that invites new ways to reflect on the events that played out across the region's landscapes via a series of temporary exhibits. Highlights include:

- The 'For Evermore' exhibition about the military cemeteries at In Flanders Fields Museum in Ypres (page 17).
- 'Talbotousians in War & Peace' exhibition at Talbot House, Poperinge (page 29), detailing the pilgrimages taken by the famous house's founder, Tubby Clayton.
- 'Reflection Points' at the Memorial Museum Passchendaele 1917 (page 27), Zonnebeke, focuses on the stories of the soldiers who died in the castle grounds.
- 'Leksems' ('Scars') is an exhibition inside Diksmuide stadhuis (page 35) exploring the scars of war still visible across the West Flemish landscape.
- Watou Art Festival showcases the work of poets and artists, spread along Watouplein in Poperinge, inspired by the theme the 'Landscape bears Witness'.

The infamous Third Battle of Ypres – also known as the Battle of Passchendaele – was one of the bloodiest battles of World War I. In the summer of 1917, fighting on Germany's east border had stopped due to the Russian Revolution and it was possible to redeploy German troops west. Faced with this imminent surge in German military strength, Britain knew it had to act quickly. Sir Douglas Haig developed a plan whose main aims were to reclaim the high ground at Passchendaele and push the Germans back from the coast in order to destroy their submarine bases, which continually threatened Britain's supply lines and the American reinforcements arriving by ship. Buoyed by success at the Battle of Messines (see box, page 34) in June, the plan was given the go-ahead and to 'clear the way' for his troops Haig ordered a massive two-week bombardment. Then on 31 July 1917, Haig sent Allied troops over the top, but a few days later the heavens opened and the worst deluge to hit the region in 30 years turned Flanders' Fields into a quagmire. Tanks got stuck, gun mechanisms jammed and crater holes that used to provide shelter from enemy fire filled with water. Men and horses drowned in the worst sections. Haig called off the attack, but stubbornly issued another on the 16 August, others on 20 and 26 September, and another on 4 October. By the time Allied forces reached Passchendaele on 6 November, 325,000 Allied soldiers and 260,000 German troops had lost their lives for the sake of five miles of land. To give a sense of the scale of the loss, it is estimated that for every square metre gained, 435 men died. Aerial photographs of Passchendaele after the war show a pockmarked lunar expanse of complete devastation.

In an attempt to gain an advantage before American troops arrived in Europe, the German Army embarked on the Lys Offensive in April 1918 and in the space of three days pushed the Allies all the way back to the outskirts of Ypres, reoccupying the land taken by the Allies during the Third Battle of Ypres. However, the effort exhausted the final reserves of the German Army and it was unable to resist the Allies' Hundred Days Offensive in August 1918. A few months later, on 11 November, the Armistice was signed in a railway carriage in Compiègne Forest, just north of Paris (see box, page 100).

German Front Line and detonated them on 19 July 1915 in an effort to break up the enemy's formation. Their lovely café is ideal for a tea and cake stop on your tour.

HARRY PATCH MEMORIAL (*Boezingestraat 97, just off the Pilkem–Langemark road*) This simple stone marks the spot where Harry Patch (the 'Last Fighting Tommy') – who died at the age of 111 in 2009 as the last surviving combat soldier of World War I – and his comrades of the 7th Battalion Duke of Cornwall's Light Infantry crossed the Steenbeek River in the early hours of 16 August 1917 (as part of the Third Battle of Ypres) to reconquer Langemark – whose church steeple can be seen in the distance – from the Germans.

VANCOUVER CORNER (*Brugseweg & Zonnebekestraat crossroads, Poelkapelle; with help*) This small garden is dominated by the statue of the **Brooding Soldier**. Carved from a single piece of solid granite it was erected in memory of the 1st Canadian Division who were wiped out by a gas attack on 24 April 1915. The ferns planted round about are meant to mimic the creeping green-tinted gas.

3

Langemark German Military Cemetery (NA/S)

LANGEMARK GERMAN MILITARY CEMETERY (DEUTSCHER SOLDATENFRIEDHOF)
(*Klerkenstraat;* w *langemark-poelkapelle.be;* ⏰ *daily; free entry;* ♿) Dotted with oak trees – the national symbol of Germany – Langemark is one of four German cemeteries left in Flanders. Originally there were 68, but many were consolidated or the soldiers' remains were reinterred back home. Hitler visited the cemetery in June 1940 while Flanders was under German occupation following the Battle of France. Inside the entrance arch, carved into oak panels, are the names of the **Student Soldiers**: university students who volunteered to join the war, but were only given six weeks' training before being sent to the Western Front – often to the worst parts.

On the other side of the gate sits a square mass grave containing the remains of 24,000 unknown soldiers and tucked at the back, behind the entrance wall, is the statue of the **Mourning Soldiers**: four slumped figures modelled on a 1918 photograph of the Reserve Infantry Regiment 238 mourning at the graveside of their comrade. The trios of basalt crosses dotted throughout the cemetery are purely for decoration. The cemetery now has a Wi-Fi hotspot and a free app you can download to explain various important locations inside the cemetery.

POPPY CENOTAPH
(*Adjacent to Langemark Cemetery*) This 7m-high memorial was forged on the cobblestones of Ypres in 2016 by an international group of blacksmiths and farriers. Surrounded by 2,106 metal poppies, it also has a ring of panels featuring their interpretation of the war.

GUYNEMER PAVILION
(*Brugseweg 126, Poelkapelle;* w *guynemerpaviljoen.be/en;* ⏰ *10.00–18.30 Wed–Sun*) This monument, which stands in the village of Poelkapelle northeast of Ypres, is dedicated to Georges Guynemer – a wartime French pilot. He belonged to an elite French Air Force corps called the Escadrille des Cigognes (Stork Squadron) and he succeeded in shooting down over 50 German fighter airplanes at a time when dogfighting tactics were still in their infancy.

Sadly, on 11 September 1917 Guynemer clambered aboard his Spad biplane for a reconnaissance mission over Ypres. He was never seen again and his body was never found. Rumours suggest he was shot down near Poelkapelle, but the land was too devastated by shelling to recover any evidence. As a nod to the name of his squadron, a bronze stork tops the monument; its wings pointing in the direction of where Guynemer is said to have crashed. Guynemer's last routine orders are carved into the stone.

ZONNEBEKE

MEMORIAL MUSEUM PASSCHENDAELE 1917 (*Berten Pilstraat 5/A;* \051 77 04 41; w *passchendaele.be;* 10.00–17.30 *daily (last entrance 16.30), closed 16 Dec–31 Jan; with audio guide adult/7–18/under 7s €11.50/6/free, combi-ticket with Talbot House (page 29) €18; audio guide for kids €2*) Inside Kasteel Zonnebeke, a 1920s mansion, this museum has a collection of weaponry, uniforms and an immersive trench 'experience' complete with corrugated-iron walkways, bunker rooms, dim lights and war-sounds soundtrack.

The new wing explains, via a large-scale model, the 100-day Battle of Passchendaele (see box, page 25) that claimed the lives of hundreds of thousands of soldiers in 1917, as well as how trench design developed over the years, with examples of how the German and British versions differed. The Remembrance Gallery houses a sculpture by New Zealand artist Helen Pollock – it's made from clay scraped from soil in Passchendaele and Coromandel (New Zealand) to remember all those that died from drowning in the atrocious mud.

Next door is the Passchendaele Memorial Park with poppy gardens dedicated to the various nationalities that fought in the battle. From here you can walk the 3km (two miles) to Tyne Cot Cemetery – they're developing a smartphone guide for the walk; ask at reception for details. There's a good café on site, as well as a play park with a model plane to entertain the kids.

TYNE COT CEMETERY (*Tynecotstraat 1;* \051 77 04 41; w *passchendaele.be;* 09.00–18.00 *daily; free entry;* with help) Tyne Cot is the world's largest Commonwealth war-grave cemetery and the final resting place for 11,961 souls. The sight of its uniform graves stretching into the distance is utterly humbling. Over 70% of them belong to unidentified British or Commonwealth soldiers and bear the words 'Known unto God'. The cemetery takes its name from a barn that once stood at the centre of this German strongpoint, and which British troops presumably thought resembled a Tyneside cottage. The Germans had a couple of blockhouses or 'pillboxes' here which they used as Advance Dressing Stations (ADS). Several have been preserved, including the one beneath the mighty Cross of Sacrifice erected in 1922. Gently climb a few of its steps, and you get a glimpse of the Germans' advantageous viewpoint

Building of Tyne Cot Cemetery (MMP/VF)

overlooking the British lines and Ypres. It was this high ground for which the British fought at the Third Battle of Ypres (see box, page 25).

85TH CANADIAN MEMORIAL AND CANADA GATE (*Passendalestraat & Canadalaan 37*) Just north of Tyne Cot Cemetery, this squat monument – the first one erected in the region – honours the 85th Canadian Infantry Battalion from Nova Scotia which suffered heavy losses during the Third Battle of Ypres.

Two minutes north, on the outskirts of Passchendaele village, the double-arch Canada Gate marks the area of fiercest fighting for the Canadian Corps during the Second Battle of Passchendaele, before they later went on to win the precious high ground at Crest Farm. A second sister gate sits on Halifax waterfront in Canada to mark the departure point of the 350,000 soldiers bound for Belgium and France.

POLYGON WOOD CEMETERY AND BUTTES NEW BRITISH CEMETERY (*Lange Dreve 5;* ⊕ *daily; free entry;* ♿) The small Polygon Wood Cemetery is named after a large wood that covered this area prior to the war. It passed back and forth during the fighting, but was finally retaken by the 9th Scottish Division on 28 September 1918.

Walk across the road, via a walled avenue, past the Cross of Sacrifice, to the Buttes New British Cemetery. Ahead of you, on the hill, is the memorial to the 5th Australian Division, who captured the wood on 26 September 1917. The cemetery contains the graves of 2,108 Commonwealth servicemen, of which 1,677 are unidentified. Also standing here is the New Zealand Memorial – a mark of respect to the 378 officers who died here between September 1917 and May 1918 and have no known grave. At the end of the road, keep a lookout for the bronze *Brothers in Arms* statue (*Lotegatstraat 26*), a memorial for the Australian Hunter Brothers, John and Jim. John buried his younger brother and was later killed in action himself.

COMMAND BUNKER (*Komenstraat, Zandvoorde;* ⊕ *daily; free entry*) Preserved by the Memorial Museum Passchendaele 1917 (page 27), this reinforced-concrete 19m-long German bunker was built in 1916 by the 3rd Company of Armierungsbatallion No 27 and used as a command post – look for the plaque they erected on the bunker wall saying so. At the time, it was situated just 6km from the Front Line. A series of six rooms can be explored.

The 5th Australian Memorial overlooks Buttes New British Cemetery (CTM/VF)

4

Poperinge, Heuvelland and Messines (Mesen)

POPERINGE

Like Veurne (page 38), Poperinge was one of the few towns to remain under Allied control throughout the war and didn't see fighting. As a result, it was a haven for soldiers travelling to and from the Front Line. Troops referred to it affectionately as 'Pops'. Talbot House, in particular, became a legendary place of respite where soldiers could take needed rest and let off steam. The compact town makes an excellent day trip from Ypres and shouldn't be missed.

GETTING THERE AND AWAY From Ypres **by car**, follow the N308 west (*13.5km; approx 20mins*). You can also get to Poperinge from Ypres **by train** (*21mins past the hour Mon–Fri, 22mins past the hour Sat–Sun; 7mins*).

TOURIST INFORMATION

Toerisme Poperinge Grote Markt 1; ℡ 057 34 66 76; w toerismepoperinge.be; ⊕ 09.00–17.00 daily, but varies in winter (check website). Narrow office in the Stadhuis basement. They sell a 34km *POProute* cycling map, which takes you past the cemeteries.

WHAT TO SEE AND DO

De Cellen (*Guido Gezellestraat*; ⊕ *06.00–22.00 daily; free entry*; ☂) Just around the corner from the Stadhuis and tucked away off the street, this courtyard is the site of a very dark chapter in British World War I history. British soldiers who refused to return to the Front Line or were caught deserting – often as a result of trauma – were held in these two cells and executed at the wooden post standing at the back of the courtyard. A priest would read them their last rites, the attending medical officer would place a white cloth over their heart and a line of six riflemen would face the accused, but only one of the guns was loaded.

Now a memorial, the cell walls have been covered with perspex to protect the graffiti carved by soldiers awaiting execution. One such man was 31-year-old Eric Poole, a first officer who developed shellshock, but was sent back to the Front and arrested two days later when he tried to escape. He was executed here on 10 December 1916 at 07.25.

Talbot House (*Gasthuisstraat 43, entrance via Pottestraat*; ℡ *057 33 32 28*; w *talbothouse.be*; ⊕ *10.00–17.30 daily, last entry 16.30; 18–65s/over 65s/7–18/ under 7s €10/9/6/free, family ticket (2 adults, 3 kids) €27*) Talbot House is a very special living museum that was established in December 1915 by the Reverend Philip Clayton – best known as 'Tubby' – and chaplain Neville Talbot as a bed and breakfast for soldiers travelling to and from the Front Line.

A bedroom in Talbot House (CS/S)

Originally from Queensland, Australia, Tubby was assigned to the 6th Division as an army chaplain and posted to the salient when World War I broke out. He visited the trenches, or 'slums' as he called them, several times and narrowly escaped death on a number of occasions. He saw first-hand the unspeakable horrors soldiers faced, so he and Talbot opened the bed and breakfast as a place of 'light, warmth and laughter', a shelter from the ugliness of war and named it after Neville's brother, Gilbert, who had died in combat. Here soldiers could make as much noise as they liked, play card games and have an undisturbed night's sleep. Indeed, the 'real sheets' room (The General's Room) was famous as the only room in the house with a bedsheet – a luxury which cost five francs and was the prize of many a card game. By the summer of 1917, it's estimated 5,000 soldiers a week were passing through the house in preparation for the Third Battle of Ypres (see box, page 25).

Tubby was a jovial landlord, famous for his love of humorous adages, such as 'Never judge a man by his umbrella, it might not be his', and several are pinned above the doorways. In the chapel, which sits on the fourth floor beneath the eaves, he baptised 50 soldiers, performed 800 confirmations and delivered communion to tens of thousands of soldiers.

The house is filled with original items, but the two most poignant artefacts are found in the hallway on the ground floor. The first is 'Friendship corner', a yellowing typed-out list from the visitors' book where soldiers would leave messages for friends, or notes asking others if they knew of their whereabouts. The second, by the original entrance, is a map of the Ypres Salient (currently a photocopy; the original is undergoing restoration). Poperinge and Ypres have been wiped away by the fingerprints of soldiers pointing to where they were stationed or had lost friends – you can even make out the smudgy bulge of the salient.

After the war, Tubby was made an honorary citizen of Poperinge. He returned to England in March 1919, accompanied by his dog Chippy, and became the vicar of All Hallows Church near the Tower of London.

Talbot House was, and will remain, a hugely important place of remembrance for World War I veterans, like Harry Patch – the last surviving soldier to have fought in the trenches during World War I – who visited the house before his death in 2009 and was able to sit in the same lounge chair he'd last sat in while talking to friends in 1917.

After your visit, volunteers are happy to make you a complimentary cup of tea or coffee in the kitchen.

Lijssenthoek Military Cemetery (*Boescheepseweg 35A;* ☏ *057 34 66 76;* w *lijssenthoek.be;* ⊕ *09.00–18.00 daily; free entry;* ♿) About 4km west of Poperinge, Lijssenthoek is the second-largest Commonwealth cemetery in the world, after Tyne Cot (page 27) with 10,784 graves. Over 8,000 of these are white-sandstone British Army headstones, as well as 300 French white crosses and 130 German stones – the last are fittingly placed under oak trees at the back. There is also a collection of Chinese graves on the far left-hand side.

From 1915 to 1920, it was known as Remy Siding and was the site of the biggest field hospital in the Ypres Salient. The low-lying information centre contains excellent information panels about the hospital, as well as databanks to search for relatives and listening points on a red wall that issue snippets of soldiers' stories. In June 2024, a new immersive experience focusing on the vital wartime role of Poperinge's train tracks is scheduled to open.

Chinese Labourers Memorial (*Cnr of Hoek Visserijmolenstraat & Sint-Jansstraat;* ⊕ *daily; free entry*) During the war, 140,000 Chinese labourers were recruited to help in the Allied effort. This statue by Yan Shuten, west of Poperinge centre, in the Busseboom area, was erected to mark the one hundredth anniversary of the location where 13 Chinese workers were killed by a German bomb on 15 November 1917.

HEUVELLAND

Unlike nearby Poperinge, this rural stretch of land south of Ypres was overrun with fighting during World War I. Opposing forces clamoured to claim the region's hills that provided observation points and views over the enemy. Many of the villages were flattened and the surrounding fields still bear the pockmarks and craters of heavy fire.

GETTING THERE AND AWAY Heuvelland is very rural and best explored **by car** or **by bike**. The tourist information office can help you arrange the latter (see below). From Ypres station take **bus** No 70 (direction Nieuwkerke) to Kemmel; journey time 26 minutes.

TOURIST INFORMATION
Toerisme Heuvelland Sint-Laurentiusplein 1, 8950 Kemmel; ☏ 057 45 04 55; e toerisme@ heuvelland.be; w toerismeheuvelland.be; ⊕ 1 Apr–15 Nov 09.30–noon & 13.00–17.00 Mon–Sat, 10.00–16.00 Sun; 16 Nov–31 Mar 09.30–noon & 13.00–16.00 Tue–Sat, 10.00–16.00 Sun. Features permanent & temporary exhibitions on the war. Sells tickets for Bayernwald (page 32); World War I-focused 85km self-drive map called *Life at the Front* with full directions; *1917 Mine Battle Route* 28km cycling map starting at Hill 60; a 7km *Craters & Mines* walking route around Wijtschate; a map for the 3.5km walk along the Messines Ridge Peace Path; & they also show a free 20 min film about the Battle of Messines (see box, page 34), called *Zero Hour,* on the first floor, featuring Bayernwald & the Pool of Peace – to help you get more out of the sites. Also stocks local wines & beers.

WHAT TO SEE AND DO
Kemmel This is the area's most central village with the best tourist

4

DID YOU KNOW?

German trenches always had duckboards placed lengthways, while the Allies laid them horizontally.

'Pool of Peace', Wijtschate (W/VF)

information centre (page 31). From here, you can organise bike, walking or guided tours to see the other sites in the region.

'Den Engel' Monument aux Soldats Français (French Soldier Memorial)

(*Kemmelberg;* ♿ *with help*) This towering 18m-high column with an angel relief stands atop Kemmelberg – a famous hill that was fought over between the French and Germans during the Battle of Lys in April 1918 because it offered extensive views towards Mesen (Messines) and Ypres (Ieper). The angel overlooks the battlefield and, lower down the slope, is an ossuary (mass grave) containing the remains of the 5,000 French soldiers who died trying to defend the elevated site.

Lettenberg Bunkers (*Lokerstraat;* ⏱ *09.00–18.00 daily; free entry*) The British built these underground command posts and sleeping quarters – situated on the other side of the hill from the 'Den Engel' monument – while the Allies had control of Kemmelberg hill. The wooden sleeping compartments collapsed, but you can still visit the reinforced-concrete bunkers.

Wijtschate This tiny village lies just 3km to the east of Kemmel and can be easily reached on foot or by bike.

Bayernwald (*Voormezelestraat;* ⏱ *10.00–18.00 daily; adult/child €4/1, but tickets from Heuvelland Tourist Office;* ♿) Roughly 1km north of Wijtschate, this elevated wooded ground 40m above sea level was won by the Germans after fierce fighting and was a key site during the Battle of Messines (see box, page 34). They developed an impregnable system of trenches, bunkers and mine shafts but today you can only see about 10% of what was there during the war. Nevertheless, it's chilling to walk the same pathways the soldiers followed. It's worth watching the *Zero Hour* documentary at the tourist office in Kemmel (page 31) before visiting.

'Pool of Peace' (Spanbroekmolen Mine Crater) (*Kruisstraat; free entry*) On 7 June 1917, the British Army detonated 19 mines under German-held land between Hill 60 (page 22) and Ploegsteert. The peaceful lily-pad-covered pool you see today was one of the craters created by the explosions. Sadly, the mine here exploded 15 seconds after the other mines and attacking soldiers were caught up

in the explosion, which created a crater over 12m deep and 129m in diameter; the pool can be found between the villages of Kemmel and Wijtschate. Interestingly, it's privately owned by Talbot House in Poperinge (page 29).

MESSINES (MESEN)

Belgium's smallest city offered crucial high ground and for the first three years of the war, the Germans held on to the Messines Ridge tightly. They lost control in June 1917 at the Battle of Messines (see box, page 34).

GETTING THERE AND AWAY From Ypres take **bus** No 72 (direction Le Bizet) to Messines; journey time 15 minutes; day pass €5.

TOURIST INFORMATION
Messines Tourist Office Markt 22; ℡ 057 22 17 14; w mesen.be; ⏰ 09.00–noon & 13.30–17.00 Mon–Thu, 09.00–noon & 13.30-16.00 Fri. Doubles as a museum (see below).

WHAT TO SEE AND DO
Historical Museum (*Markt 1; ℡ 057 22 17 14; same hours as tourist information (see above; free entry*) Artefacts from the former historical museum have been rehoused in the tourist information centre (see above) and combined with video panels and timelines explaining the Battle of Messines (see box, page 34). Inside, you can download the 'Messines Walk' app, which follows the progress of the New Zealand troops during the Battle of Messines using pictures and sound snippets. You can download it in English for Android on Google Play Store and for iPhone and iPad at the Apple App Store. Outside the museum is a new statue commemorating the Christmas Day Truce (see box, below) between Allied and German forces.

CHRISTMAS TRUCE

On Christmas Eve 1914, near Plugstreet/Ploegsteert, Ypres, soldiers of the British Expeditionary Force heard German troops singing *Silent Night* in their trenches and joined in. On Christmas Day, German soldiers emerged from their trenches, calling out 'Merry Christmas' and Allied soldiers met them on No Man's Land to exchange gifts of cigarettes and plum puddings, take photographs and even play impromptu games of football. It was never repeated – the chivalry quashed by officers who feared it would undermine the soldiers' ability to fight. Captain Bruce Bairnsfather – a prominent British cartoonist of the war – described the incident in his diary:

I wouldn't have missed that unique and weird Christmas Day for anything…I spotted a German officer, some sort of lieutenant I should think, and being a bit of a collector, I intimated to him that I had taken a fancy to some of his buttons…I brought out my wire clippers and, with a few deft snips, removed a couple of his buttons and put them in my pocket. I then gave him two of mine in exchange…

Christmas Truce Memorial, Messines
(IB/WC)

The aim of this week-long attack, 7–14 June 1917, was to overwhelm German defences and capture the Messines Ridge, a key section of high ground that overlooked the fields south of Ypres. British General Herbert Plumer had been preparing for the attack 18 months in advance. 'Sappers' had been digging tunnels that stretched under German lines and, at times, they'd meet counter-tunnellers digging towards British lines – hand-to-hand combat would break out underground.

Twenty-two mines – over 600 tonnes of explosives – were placed at the end of the shafts and on the eve of the attack Plumer said the following to his staff: 'Gentlemen, we may not make history tomorrow, but we shall certainly change the geography.' At 03.10 that morning, 19 of the mines safely detonated and the German line was blown to smithereens – over 10,000 soldiers were killed outright. It's rumoured the explosion was so loud it was heard by war-cabinet minister Lloyd George in Downing Street, London.

Allied troops advanced, keeping up a barrage of gunfire, and within hours British and New Zealand troops had conquered the ridge. The battle is considered one of the biggest successes of the Allied forces, but it was the precursor to the larger and bloodier Third Battle of Ypres (see box, page 25).

Island of Ireland Peace Park (*Armentiersesteenweg;* ⏰ *09.00–17.00 Mon–Fri; guided tours possible, ask tourist office; free entry;* ♿) Just south of Messines village centre, this memorial park is dedicated to all Irish soldiers killed or wounded during World War I. Its main feature is a 33m-high tower built in traditional 8th-century Irish style and made from stones reclaimed from a demolished workhouse in County Westmeath in Ireland. Amazingly, the inside of the tower only sees light on the 11th hour of the 11th day in November thanks to a trick of design. Notice the rings embedded into the floor: they're spaced at 10, 16 and 36m to symbolise the three Irish Divisions who fought. Three stone tablets marking the men they lost are posted to the right of the entrance path.

Messines Ridge British Cemetery (*Nieuwkerkestraat;* ⏰ *daily; free entry;* ♿) When the Armistice was signed, graves from numerous impromptu burial plots in the surrounding area were moved here for proper interment. Today, there are 1,534 Commonwealth graves, of which 957 are unidentified.

At the entrance is the Messines Ridge New Zealand Memorial to the Missing, carved with the names of 839 soldiers who died in the Battle of Messines (see box, above) and have no known grave.

The Irish Round Tower at Ireland Peace Park, dedicated to the soldiers of Ireland who died or went missing during World War I (ET)

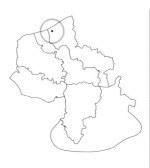

5

Diksmuide, Veurne and Nieuwpoort

DIKSMUIDE

Wandering around Diksmuide's pleasant Grote Markt listening to the golden-oldie tunes being softly piped out across the square, it's hard to imagine the intense conflicts played out here during World War I. From the very start, the town became embroiled in the Battle of Yser, which effectively dismantled Germany's Schlieffen Plan and established the boundaries of the Front Line that would barely move for the next four years. The main sites of interest are the Yser Tower peace monument and the preserved Dodengang trenches, but do take the time to buy a couple of *Ijzerbollen* – local custard-filled creations.

GETTING THERE AND AWAY

By car From Ypres follow the N369 north (*22.6km; approx 30mins*); from Veurne follow the N36 westwards (*17.4km; approx 20mins*); from Brugge follow the N31 south and merge with the E40 (direction Ostend/Oostende), take exit 4 (direction Middelkerke) and follow the N369 south (*50km; approx 47mins*).

By train Ypres via Kortrijk and Lichtervelde (*39mins past the hour daily; 2hrs 11mins*); Bruges via Lichtervelde (*7mins past the hour daily; 43mins*); Ghent (*51mins past the hour daily; 59mins*); Veurne (*3mins past the hour daily; 11mins*).

TOURIST INFORMATION

Diksmuide Tourist Office Grote Markt 6; ☎ 051 79 30 50; w tourism.diksmuide.be; ⊕ 1 Oct–31 Mar 10.00–12.30 & 13.30–16.00 Mon–Sat, 1 Apr–30 Sept 09.30–17.00 daily. Sells the *Ijzer Front* 79km car route map in English, which takes

you on a tour of the sites & memorials associated with the Battle of Yser (see box, page 40). They also sell the *Ijzer 14–18* cycling map (41km), which takes you past Vladslo Cemetery, the trenches & Yser Tower.

WHAT TO SEE AND DO

Museum on the Yser (Museum aan de IJzer) (*Ijzerdijk 49;* ☎ *051 50 02 86;* w *aandeijzer.be;* ⊕ *Oct–Mar 09.00–17.00 Mon–Fri, 10.00–17.00 Sat–Sun; Apr–Sep 09.00–18.00 Mon–Fri, 10.00–18.00 Sat–Sun; adult/7–17/under 7s €9/5/free;* ♿ *with help, some floors off-limits*) The cross-shaped Yser Tower protrudes 84m above the horizon; a giant, and defiant, monument to peace. Erected in 1965, its base is inscribed with the words 'No More War' in four languages and its 22 levels are dedicated to the retelling of the war (and a bit on Belgian politics too). Start at the very top of the tower, on the 22nd floor, which offers sweeping 360-degree views of the landscape. The museum provides tablets that allow visitors to scan the

The cross-shaped Yser Tower (NA/S)   *Trenches at Dodengang (EA/S)*

horizon and discover traces of war. It's really useful for seeing the transformation from the wartime landscape to that of today. The tablet also includes a kid's tour, giving children the opportunity to search for historical characters in the landscape. From there, work your way down, experiencing the smell of mustard and chlorine gas (level 15) and dim and frightening recreated trenches (level 3), before entering the Crypt, where you can download an app on your smartphone that explains the politics and symbolism of the site.

There's also the **PAX gate**, a monumental archway built in 1950 from the ruined remains of the first Yser Tower which was built in 1928 but blown up on 15 March 1946 by pro-French Belgian military members who opposed the growing strength of the Flemish Independence Movement. The tower was a target because it contains the graves of eight leading Flemish freedom-fighters.

Passing by the gate, you enter a compound where the first tower stood – button #4 on the right-hand wall gives an explanation of its various elements in English. What's most important to notice is the inscription on the eight freedom-fighters' graves: AVV, VVK 'Alles voor Vlaanderen, Vlaanderen voor Kristus' (All for Flanders, Flanders for Christ). Prior to World War I, the Flemish were at a distinct social disadvantage to their French-speaking Wallonian countrymen: there were no Flemish schools, and if you couldn't speak French you couldn't qualify as an officer. The discrepancies angered Flemish soldiers, who began to question why they should fight and die for their country when the government would place a tombstone bearing a French motto on their grave. The Flemish Independence Movement came up with the above.

Dodengang (*Ijzerdijk 65;* ☏*051 50 53 44;* w *dodengang.be;* ◷ *1 Apr–15 Nov 10.00–18.00 daily, last entry 17.00; 16 Nov–31 Mar 09.30–16.00 Tue & Thu, last entry 15.00; adult/6–18/under 6s €6/4/free;* ♿ *with help*) Located 2km north of the Yser Tower, this 400m stretch of preserved trenches has been carefully maintained 'Lest we forget'. Allied troops called it the Trench of Death and spent four years here bravely holding the Front Line.

Vladslo War Cemetery (*Houtlandstraat 3, 8600 Vladso-Diksmuide;* ◷ *daily; free entry*) Over 25,000 soldiers are buried at this German war cemetery, which also contains the hugely moving *Grieving Parents* sculpture created by Käthe Kollwitz whose 18-year-old son, Peter, was killed in the war.

To get there you can cycle or call the Belbus (☏ *059 56 52 56*) 2 hours prior to the time you want to travel. It'll pick you up from an agreed spot and drop you on Houtlandstraat, a 400m walk from the cemetery. Alternatively, you can call a taxi (*Taxi Charlie;* ☏*0475 58 62 29*).

Käthe Kollwitz' Grieving Parents *sculpture (W/VF)*

VEURNE

Just four miles from the French border and the North Sea coastline, Veurne – or Furnes as it's known in French – boasts one of Flanders's most authentic market squares because the town was situated 9km from the Front Line during World War I and, as a result, many of its 16th-century buildings avoided destruction.

GETTING THERE AND AWAY From Ypres **by car**, follow the N8 northwest (*31km; approx 35mins*). From Bruges R30 follow signs for the E40 and follow it west for 33.5km, then take exit 1a (*54km; approx 42mins*). If travelling **by train**, Bruges via Lichtervelde (*7mins past the hour daily; 54mins*); Ypres–Kortrijk–Lichtervelde–Veurne (*39mins past the hour daily; 2hrs 20mins*).

TOURIST INFORMATION

Veurne Tourist Office Grote Markt 29; ☏ 058 33 55 31; w veurne.be; ⏰ 1 Apr–15 Nov 09.00–17.00 Mon–Fri, 10.00–17.00 Sat–Sun; 16 Nov–31 Mar 09.00–17.00 Mon–Fri, 13.00–17.00 Sat–Sun. Large, modern office inside the Landhuis with information covering the whole of West Flanders & an interactive museum about the area & the war.

WHAT TO SEE AND DO

Stadhuis (Town Hall) (*Grote Markt 29; ☏ 058 33 55 31; ⏰ 1 Apr–11 Nov 09.00–17.00 Mon–Fri, 10.00–17.00 Sat–Sun (last entrance 16.30); 12 Nov–31 Mar*

The King Albert I Monument at Nieuwpoort has a diameter of 30m (MPP/VF)

09.00–17.00 Mon–Fri, 13.00–17.00 Sat–Sun) A pretty little thing tucked away in the western corner of the Grote Markt, this consists of two parts: the Stadhuis – easily recognisable thanks to its colonnade decorated with golden angels on a blue background – and the adjacent Landhuis. They served as headquarters of the Belgian Army during World War I – it was here King Albert I met Britain's King George V in the Albert Hall and Karel Cogge's flooding plan was approved (see box, page 40) – and narrowly avoided destruction. The main attraction is the **Free the Fatherland – Life Behind the Front** (w *vrijvaderland.be; adult/65+/7–18/ under 7s €4/3/2/free*) multimedia museum that focuses on what daily life was like in unoccupied Belgium.

NIEUWPOORT

This chic coastal town was embroiled in the Battle of the Yser – part of the First Battle of Ypres – when its dam gates were opened to flood the Flemish plains and halt the German advancement.

GETTING THERE AND AWAY If travelling by **train** or **tram**, travel first to Ostende via Roeslaere (*1hr 30mins*), then catch the *kusttram* (w *delijn.be/dekusttram)* west to Nieuwpoort (*20mins*).

TOURIST INFORMATION
Nieuwport Tourist Offices Marktplein 7 & Hendrikaplein 11; w visit-nieuwpoort.be;

⏰ 09.30–12.30 & 13.30–17.00 Mon–Sun, Jul & Aug 09.30–18.00 daily

Intent on completing the first phase of the Schlieffen Plan – to capture Paris – the German Army advanced rapidly towards the Belgian coastline during the first few months of World War I. To halt their advance, Belgian troops established a Front Line 22 miles behind the Yser Canal, which ran from Nieuwpoort to Arras in France. However, during the Battle of the Yser the Germans crossed the water and it was feared the Allies were on the verge of losing their hold in Belgium. (The tourist office publishes a car route map that takes you past monuments and memorials associated with the battle; see page 39.)

Karel Cogge, a Veurne local and superintendent of the Northern Waterways, suggested they open the sluice gates at Nieuwpoort (page 39) and slowly flood the area to halt the Germans. The idea was approved and on 26 and 29 October 1914 the gates were raised by Nieuwpoort skipper Hendrik Geeraert, flooding the polders. His actions had single-handedly prevented Belgium becoming fully occupied and ended the Germans' 'Race to the Sea' for control of Calais and Dunkerque. In recognition of his services, Cogge was knighted in the Landhuis by King Albert I. Two paintings of him can be found in the Mayor's Cabinet of the Stadhuis and the Albert Hall of the Landhuis. His bust stands on Noordstraat. Geeraert was later awarded the Order of Leopold and celebrated on the 1,000 Belgian franc banknote during the 1950s.

WHAT TO SEE AND DO

Ganzepoot Dam ('Goose Foot' Lock Complex) (*Kustweg 2;* \ *058 23 07 33;* w *westfrontnieuwpoort.be;* ◔ *10.00–17.00 daily (last entrance 16.00); adults/7–25/ under 6s €7/5/free*) The Yser River reaches the sea at Nieuwpoort via this complex of locks. In 1914, an idea was hatched to open the sluices and flood the Yser Plain to prevent the German advancement towards French ports and British supply lines – and it worked (see box, above). The hyper-modern visitor centre under the monument features a computer game that gives you an impression of how the sluice gates were opened.

King Albert I Monument (*Kustweg*) This circular, colonnaded monument was built in 1938 in honour of the king, who commanded the Belgian Army throughout the war. It's possible to walk around the top of the monument and survey the views over the Yser Plain.

Ramskapelle Belgian Military Cemetery (*Ramskapellestraat 38, at the crossroads of the N367, running east from Nieuwpoort, & the N356;* ◔ *daily; free entry*) This cemetery contains the graves of 635 Belgian soldiers, of which 400 are unidentified. The majority died in the 1914 Battle of the Yser.

6

Mons

The elegant town of Mons lies in the French-speaking region of Wallonia, about 65km southwest of Brussels, and is best remembered for the Battle of Mons (see box, below). The city was captured almost immediately by the Germans and remained under their control until the Canadians liberated it on 11 November 1918. Poignantly, it was here that the first and last British soldiers died during World War I – you can see their graves at Saint-Symphorien Cemetery (page 43).

GETTING THERE AND AWAY

If you're staying in Ypres, drive **by car** southeast following the A19 towards Kortrijk, taking the E403 south to Tournai, picking up the E42 and then the E19 to Mons (*109km; approx 1hr*). **Trains** depart daily every half an hour from Ypres with a change at Bruxelles-Zuid/Gare-du-Midi (*1hr 10mins; €31.60 return*).

TOURIST INFORMATION

Mons Tourist Office Grand Place 27; 065 33 55 80; w visitmons.co.uk; ⏲ 09.30–17.30 daily

THE BATTLE OF MONS

The Battle of Mons was the British Expeditionary Force's (BEF) first engagement of World War I. The German Army had been advancing across the Franco-Belgian border on its first stages of the Schlieffen Plan and on 23 August 1914 the British stepped in to block the outermost wing that threatened to encircle the Allies (particularly the French). Short on time, 80,000 BEF soldiers went up against 160,000 Germans, who also had twice the number of artillery guns (600). Despite this, the BEF made a promising start: they hounded the Germans with rifle fire so intense and consistent the Germans believed they were using machine guns. There were numerous instances of bravery, including that of Lieutenant Maurice James Dease and Private Sydney Frank Godley (page 44). However, by 15.00 that day British troops were ordered to retreat to the south of Mons and eventually they, and the French, were pushed back for the next two weeks. Nevertheless, the battle was hailed as a success in Britain. Troops had been heavily outnumbered yet inflicted many more casualties than they sustained and they were able to escape. They'd also succeeded in protecting the French from being outflanked and delayed the Germans for a crucial 48 hours – not bad for an army that hadn't seen action since the Crimean War over 60 years before!

Graves of soldiers from the 4th Battalion of the Middlesex Regiment, Saint-Symphorien Cemetery (WBT-JPR)

WHAT TO SEE AND DO

MEMORIAL PLAQUES, TOWN HALL (*Grand Place 22*) Happily, Mons's Gothic Town Hall escaped destruction during the war. You can only visit the interior by prior appointment (consult the tourist office; page 41), but the feature of most interest is mounted on the exterior walls. Beside the entrance are two bronze plaques: one is dedicated to the 5th Royal Irish Lancers who took part in the two battles of Mons in 1914 and 1918; the other is dedicated to the 3rd Canadian Division that took part in the liberation fighting in November 1918.

MONS CEMETERY (*Chemin de la Procession; take N6 north towards Brussels & after 600m turn right on to Chemin de la Procession, the cemetery is 1km on the left;* ⏲ *09.00–16.00 daily; free entry;* ♿) The communal cemetery was extended by the Germans and is now part of the town cemetery. Commonwealth, German, as well as Belgian, French, Italian, Russian and Romanian soldiers are buried here.

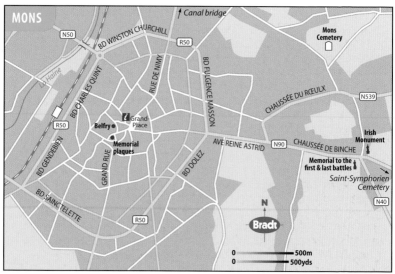

SAINT-SYMPHORIEN CEMETERY (CIMITIÈRE SAINT-SYMPHORIEN) (*Rue Nestor Dehon; follow N90 2km east of Mons towards Charleroi, turn right off N90 on to N564 & Rue Nestor Dehon; the cemetery lies 200m along on the right-hand side; ⏱ sunrise to sunset, daily; free entry*) Praised as the most beautiful on the Western Front, this leafy cemetery contains an equal number of German and British graves of soldiers killed in action during the battles of Mons; many belonged to the 4th Battalion of the Middlesex Regiment. There are a few notable graves to look out for: that of Private John Parr, the first British soldier to die in the conflict. On 21 August 1914, Parr's battalion sent him on a bicycle patrol near Casteau-Maisières and their group was surprised by a German patrol and 20-year-old Parr was hit by gunfire. Private George Ellison of the 5th Irish Lancers was killed on 11 November 1918 and was the last casualty of the war. Also, look out for Lieutenant Maurice James Dease (page 44) who won the Victoria Cross for his bravery during the Battle of Mons.

MEMORIAL TO THE FIRST AND LAST BATTLES (*On the N90 & N40 crossroads*) East of town, this twin-pillar memorial stands in honour of those who fought in the First Battle of Mons in 1914 and the Canadian regiments who fought for 60 hours non-stop to reclaim the city in November 1918.

IRISH MONUMENT (*On the N90 & N40 crossroads*) Just across the road from the first-and-last battles memorial listed above, this Celtic cross honours the Royal Irish Rifles who fell at the First Battle of Mons.

CANAL BRIDGE (*N6 towards Nimy & Brussels, Rue de Viaduc/Ave de la Joyeuse Entrée*) If you drive, or walk, north of the city you'll cross the Canal du Centre. Standing on this bridge, you're overlooking salient ground – the British dug in on one side, Germans on the other. Looking upstream you'll see an old railway bridge

Canal Bridge (pj/S)

in the distance. It was this bridge that Lieutenant Maurice James Dease and Private Sydney Frank Godley, of the 4th Royal Fusiliers, defended with machine guns. Twenty-four-year-old Dease was shot five times and died in the ambulance on the way to a dressing station; Godley took over the gun and dismantled it before he was captured by the Germans. Godley survived and died shortly after World War II. Both were awarded the Victoria Cross for their bravery.

THE ANGELS OF MONS

Legend has it that on the night of 23 August 1914, during the Battle of Mons, the British 7th Bremen Regiment, who had held Spiennes, found themselves almost encircled by German forces and annihilation seemed certain. However, as midnight struck, angel archers descended from the sky and held off the Germans, allowing the British to escape under the cover of darkness.

For years, conspiracy theories abounded as to whether this story was true. In fact, Welsh journalist and author Arthur Machen created the legend. He had heard reports of the fighting at the First Battle of Mons and how German troops had far outnumbered the British and realised how similar it was to the tale of phantom bowmen saving soldiers in the Battle of Agincourt. He submitted the piece as a short story, but his editor at *The Evening News* unintentionally ran it as a proper news feature because, up until then, Machen had written a number of factual pieces about the war.

An illustration of the so-called 'Angels of Mons' halting the German advance *(C/A)*

Part Three

FRANCE

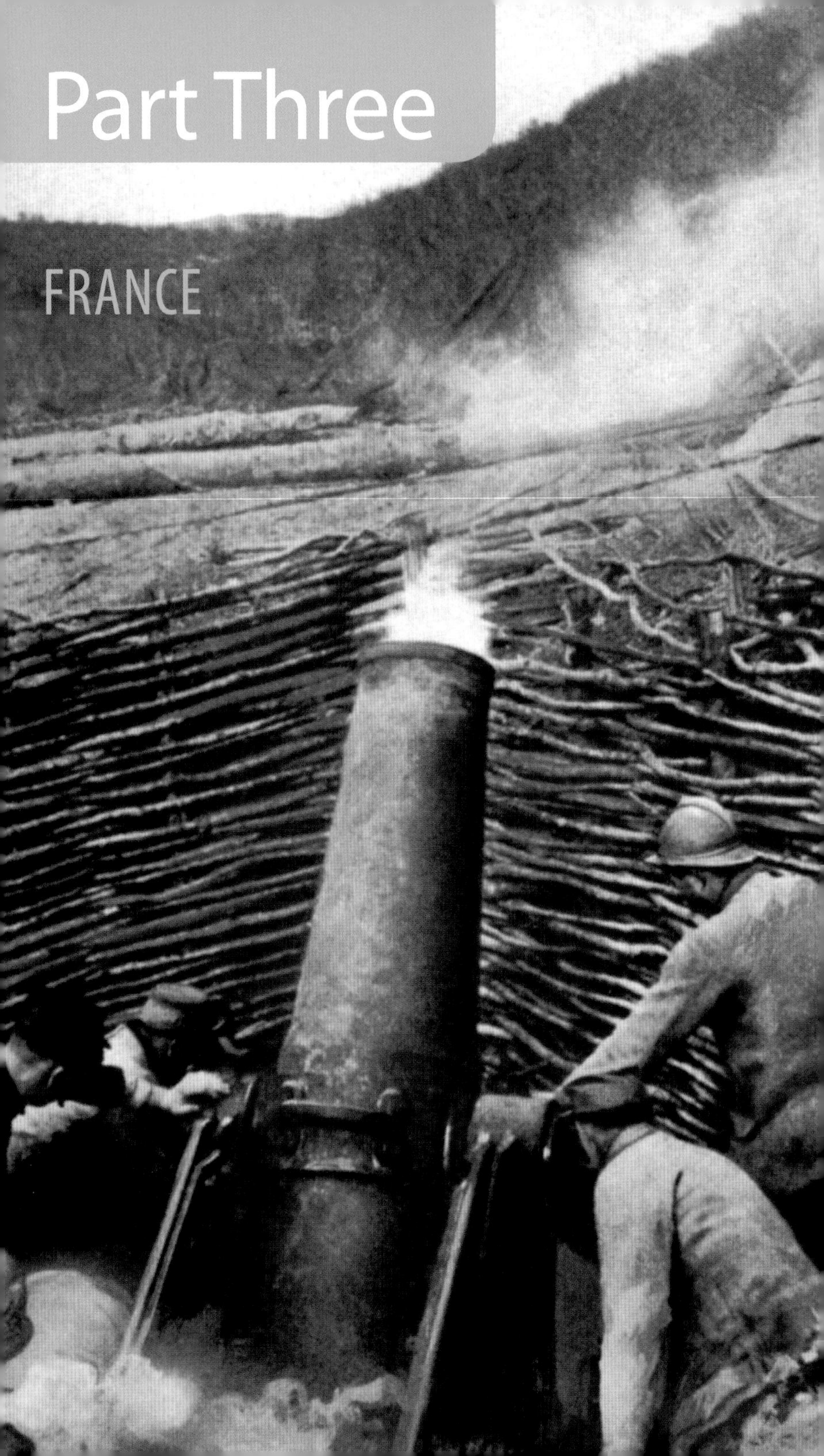

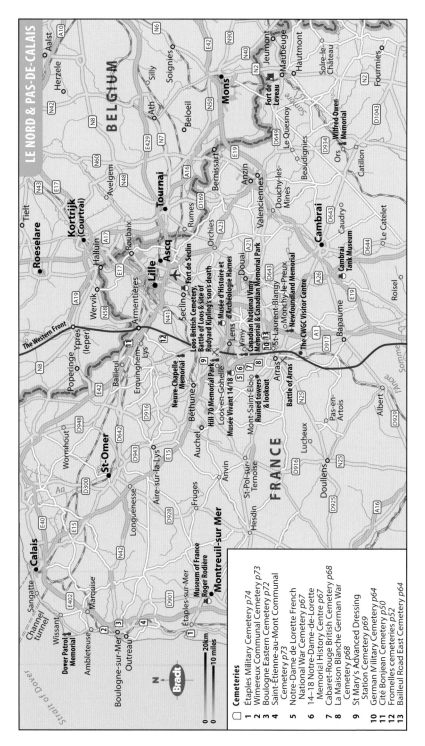

Cemeteries

1   Étaples Military Cemetery *p74*
2   Wimereux Communal Cemetery *p73*
3   Boulogne Eastern Cemetery *p72*
4   Saint-Étienne-au-Mont Communal
     Cemetery *p73*
5   Notre-Dame de Lorette French
     National War Cemetery *p67*
6   14–18 Notre-Dame-de-Lorette
     Memorial History Centre *p67*
7   Cabaret-Rouge British Cemetery *p68*
8   La Maison Blanche German War
     Cemetery *p68*
9   St Mary's Advanced Dressing
     Station Cemetery *p69*
10   German Military Cemetery *p64*
11   Cité Bonjean Cemetery *p50*
12   Fromelles cemeteries *p52*
13   Bailleul Road East Cemetery *p64*

Le Nord and Lille

LILLE

In 2016, the Nord-Pas de Calais and Picardy regions merged and were renamed Hauts-de-France. Lille is the regional capital and it played a major role from the outset of war by tricking the Germans into accepting it as a neutral or 'open city' to protect its industrial prowess. The Allies likewise refrained from bombing it throughout the war. However, on 3 October 1914, with the opposing armies attempting to outflank each other in their 'race to the sea', the Germans destroyed an entire section when the French desperately tried to defend the city. Lille capitulated on 13 October and wasn't liberated by British troops until 17 October 1918. By then, the Germans had inflicted considerable damage to the industrial and transport infrastructure.

Only a few kilometres behind the Western Front, Lille proved an ideal base for the Allies to contact a **Resistance movement** – a renegade collection of businessmen and petty criminals, led by Eugène Jacquet – whose members did everything they could to make life for the Germans as difficult as possible. In March 1915, they managed to return a pilot, whose plane had been shot down, back to Britain and a few months later he flew over Lille dropping leaflets mocking Governor Von Heinrich. Sadly, shortly after, the network's 200 members were betrayed and arrested. Jacquet and his closest comrades were shot on 22 September 1915 and the others were either sent to prison or deported. It's just one example of the bravery exhibited by young men during World War I.

GETTING THERE AND AWAY If crossing **by car** via Dunkerque take the A25 direct to Lille, or join the A16 if using the ferry to Calais (*74km; 1hr 30mins*). The same applies if you're using the Eurotunnel, though the A26 is that much closer. From Ypres, join the N365 south, then join the N58 towards Armentières, then the A25/E42 towards Lille (*40km; 40mins*). Remember, Lille is Rijsel in Flemish and will change on the road signs. Select Eurostar **trains** stop at Lille en route to Brussels.

TOURIST INFORMATION
Lille Tourist Office Palais Rihour, Pl Rihour; ☏ 03 59 57 94 00; e contact@lilletourism.com; w lilletourism.com; ⊕ 09.30–18.00 Mon–Sat, 10.00–16.30 Sun & public holidays

WHAT TO SEE AND DO Lille's imposing **war memorial** on Place Rihour is built on the site of the old City Hall, which burnt down in 1916. Its post-war design comprises allegories: one evokes the fate of 30 hostages, who in July 1915 were held to coerce the townsfolk into working for the occupying army; a further 131 were deported in November 1916.

Born into an aristocratic family of fading fortunes at Saint-Amand-les-Eaux in 1880, Louise de Bettignies was forced to earn a living working as a governess for wealthy European families. After fleeing Lille in 1914 to take up nursing the wounded at Saint-Omer, Louise, a brilliant linguist, enrolled in the British Secret Service using the pseudonym Alice Dubois. Marie-Léonie Vanhoutte, aka Charlotte Lameron, from Roubaix, soon joined her. The 'Alice Network' had 80 agents enlisted in Lille and ran extended operations to Cambrai, Valenciennes and Saint-Quentin in Picardy, monitoring troop movements and locating military depots. The agents also helped Allied soldiers escape to Holland, which was neutral at the time.

However, on 24 September 1915, Marie-Léonie was caught in a trap and later, on 21 October, so too was Louise. The death sentence in each case was reduced to forced labour, but on 27 September 1918 Louise died in Cologne from pneumonia which her jailers refused to treat. The cross that marked her temporary grave is now at the French National War Cemetery at Notre-Dame de Lorette (page 67). Her former home on rue Louise de Bettignies in Saint-Amand-les-Eaux was once a museum but is now a resource centre devoted to the emancipation of women. Its exterior features a large portrait of her.

At the top of Boulevard Carnot, on the road to the Greater Lille towns of Roubaix and Tourcoing, a statue depicts a soldier kissing the hand of **Louise de Bettignies** – boss of probably the biggest spy network of World War I (see box, above).

Roubaix suffered terribly under the Germans, who remained there from 14 October 1914 to 17 October 1918. It was only thanks to Dutch and American philanthropists that the industrial town, which relied heavily on imported resources, averted famine. A strong Resistance produced *L'Oiseau de France,* a newspaper containing reports from France and England, but the paper was shut down following a flurry of arrests in 1916.

Lille's war memorial, Place Rihour (V/WC)

SECLIN

Seclin is a town with Gallo-Roman roots, situated 10km south of Lille. Like Lille, it was occupied by the Germans during the war.

GETTING THERE AND AWAY From Lille **by car**, follow the D549 south direct to Seclin (*10.2km; approx 21mins*). You can also get here **by train**. Trains depart Lille Flandres every 30 minutes (*12mins*).

TOURIST INFORMATION
Seclin Tourist Office 70 Rue Roger Bouvry; 03 20 90 12 12; w seclin-tourisme.fr; ⏱ 14.00–17.30 Mon, 09.00–12.30 & 14.00–17.30 Tue–Fri, 09.00–12.30 Sat

WHAT TO SEE AND DO

Fort de Seclin (*Chemin du Fort;* `03 20 97 14 18;` **w** *fortseclin.com;* ⊕ *Feb–early Nov; guided tours Apr–11 Nov 14.00 & 16.00 Sat & Sun; adult/child €6/5)* The Fort de Seclin was built in 1874 and was originally meant to join a line of 400 planned forts stretching from Nice to Dunkerque and between the North Sea and the Swiss border. It became part of Lille's 21 military posts. It didn't see much action, although a

Fort de Seclin (@FS)

regiment of soldiers from the German state of Bavaria, stationed at the occupied fort, did take part in the Battle of Fromelles in July 1916 (page 51). It was liberated in October 1918 by the British 6th Battalion The King's Liverpool Regiment and used as a field hospital until 1920.

Father of five Didier Boniface then bought the abandoned fort in 1995 for 1 franc (!) and filled it with his collection of military uniforms, medals, 'képis' and other peaked caps, as well as wagons, tanks and artillery, including the famous 13-pounder quick-firing field gun which was used by the British Royal Horse Artillery at the outbreak of World War I. It now houses the 14–18 Museum with the officers' barracks converted into visitor accommodation. A 2-hour guided culture and nature tour, often led by Madame Boniface, is available from Easter to early November: check dates.

Every year in mid-October, the fort celebrates its liberation by an English regiment with a re-enactment day called the Journée du Poilu. Over the weekend, visitors can visit the museum and gain an insight into camp life and gun shooting.

To get to Fort de Seclin **by car**, turn off the A1 Lille–Paris at junction 19.

ARMENTIÈRES

Sometimes nicknamed 'The Nursery' given its gentle surroundings, Armentières became, for the British during World War I, one of the best-known towns on the Western Front, made famous by a caustic British song entitled 'Mademoiselle from Armentières'.

GETTING THERE AND AWAY From Lille **by car**, take the A25/E42 west towards Dunkerque and turn off at the junction with the D945 and follow the signs for Armentières (*20km; approx 25mins*). **Trains** depart from Lille Flandres direct to Armentières (*15mins*).

TOURIST INFORMATION

Armentières Tourist Office 4 Rue Robert Schuman; `03 61 76 21 85;` **w** rex-tourisme.com; ⊕ 10.00–18.00 Tue–Sat, 14.00–18.00 1st Sun of month. Housed inside the local history museum, Rex (adult/under 8s €4/free), they also sell local products & rent electric bikes.

> **LOCAL TOUCH**
>
> Fancy a tour by a local volunteer? Check out **Greeters** (**w** *greeters62.com*), part of a worldwide network of locals who volunteer to show you around their hometown for free. They also operate in the Picardy region.

Neuve-Chapelle Memorial (SS)

WHAT TO SEE AND DO

Cité Bonjean Cemetery (*Av Roger Salengro, just off the D945 before entering Erquinghem-Lys;* w *ww1cemeteries.com/cite-bonjean-military-cemetery;* ⊙ *daily; free entry;* ♿ *with some difficulty.*) This vast expanse of headstones is the final resting place of 2,643 soldiers of various nationalities. The cemetery was opened in 1914 and then used as a civilian cemetery because the one in nearby Bizet was too exposed to bombardment. The Cité Bonjean New Zealand Memorial is just one of the seven memorials in France and Belgium built in memory of the New Zealanders who fell on the Western Front.

Erquinghem-Lys Situated just a few kilometres from the Front, Erquinghem-Lys was for most of the war a forward base occupied by Commonwealth troops. However, in April 1918, the town was razed to the ground during a final attempt by the Germans to reach the North Sea. The **Churchyard Military Cemetery** contains 558 Commonwealth burials (eight of them unidentified) and 130 German burials. One unidentified Russian serviceman is also buried in the extension, which, like a number in the area, was designed by Sir Herbert Baker.

Getting there The village of Erquinghem-Lys is a 10-minute drive southwest of Armentières along the D945. While you can get from Lille to Armentières by métro and bus (métro line 2 to St-Philibert, then bus No 77 or 79), it is quicker to take the TER train and then catch a taxi from Armentières to Erquinghem-Lys.

Musée d'Ercan (*Rue de L'issue;* ℡ *03 20 48 05 22;* ⊙ *Mar–mid Nov 15.00–18.30 Sun, or by appointment* e *jack.thorpe@orange.fr; free entry*) Run by the local history association, it was built to commemorate a Front Line attack in 1917 – dubbed 'Dicky's Dash' – by a company of the Liverpool Scottish led by Captain Alan Dickinson MC.

Neuve-Chapelle Memorial (*Route d'Estaires (RD 947), 800m west-southwest of Neuve Chapelle village & 20km west of Lille*) Flanked by two tigers and surmounted by a Lotus Flower, the Star of India and the Imperial Crown, this high column of white stone is the only place of remembrance on the Western Front to commemorate the enormous sacrifice made by Indian soldiers during World War I.

Inaugurated in 1927, and tucked between two weeping willows, the memorial was the work of Sir Herbert Baker, the British architect who also designed Tyne Cot War Cemetery, Ypres (page 27). It was built in honour of the Indian soldiers of World War I. Beneath the epitaph 'To the honour of the Army of India which fought in France and Belgium, 1914–1918…' are listed, by regiment, the names of the 4,857 soldiers who were reported missing in action. A bronze plaque completes the list with the names of the 206 Indian prisoners of war who died in Germany. The front gate was removed in 2022 for renovation by the Commonwealth War Graves Commission.

The memorial is a reminder of the role the wider Commonwealth played in World War I. When the British were severely tested by the fighting in the summer of 1914, they called upon military units already established in India. The first reinforcements landed in Marseilles in September 1914 and were soon transported to Flanders. The Sikhs, Ghurkhas, Punjabis and other Indians who arrived, were ill-prepared for the harsh conditions in the trenches, and suffered from a lack of warm clothing and food. In March 1915, during the Battle of Aubers Ridge, they took part in the Battle of Neuve-Chapelle, where more than 4,000 of their comrades perished.

FROMELLES

Situated some 16km west of Lille, the village of Fromelles became the scene of bitter fighting in 1916 when the British High Command launched a major diversionary offensive on the village, which sat behind German lines, to prevent the Germans moving troops to the Battle of the Somme (see box, page 80).

In July 1916, the offensive deteriorated into the bloody **Battle of Fromelles**, which took place in open fields just northwest of the village. In just one night of fighting, the Australians sustained 5,533 casualties in what is described as the worst 24 hours in the military history of their country. The British counted 1,547 casualties – dead, wounded or captured – and approximately 1,600 injured or dead German soldiers

> ### TOMB OF THE UNKNOWN WARRIOR
>
> In 1916, the Reverend David Railton, a locally based chaplain, visited the Churchyard and Suffolk Regiment military cemeteries at La Rolanderie Farm and saw the epitaph 'A Soldier of the Great War/Known unto God' carved on crosses. He vowed to provide a less stark way of honouring the dead once the fighting was over.
>
> His promise was fulfilled in 1920 when, as part of British commemorations, one of six bodies exhumed from major battle areas on the Western Front was taken to Westminster Abbey on 11 November and interred in what became known as the Tomb of the Unknown Warrior. It is now one of the most visited war graves in the world and thereafter the idea of a symbolic tomb quickly spread worldwide. In France, La Tombe du Soldat Inconnu was placed in the Arc de Triomphe in Paris on 11 November 1920 as well.

were also recorded. Many were teenagers, in what was probably a fruitless exercise because archive material strongly suggests the Germans already knew the attack was a ruse to divert attention from the Somme.

GETTING THERE AND AWAY Fromelles is served by the Lille metropolitan transport network (Ilévia), but **car** is a much easier way to reach this small commune. Take the A25/E42 west out of Lille (towards Dunkerque), branch left on to the N41 (towards La Bassée), then first right on to the D141 (*17.2km; approx 20mins*). The closest accommodation is in Lille, which is also the main source of information (page 47).

TOURIST INFORMATION
Fromelles Tourist Office   Head Office: Rue Faidherbe 1158, Fournes-en-Weppes; 03 20 50 63 85; w weppes-tourisme.com; ⊕ 09.00–noon & 14.00–17.00 Mon–Fri, 09.30–noon Sat. This is part of the Weppes Tourist Office, there is also a small office in the town which is not open every day.

WHAT TO SEE AND DO
VC Corner Australian Cemetery (*Rue Delval, on the D22C, 2km northwest of Fromelles on the road to Sailly-sur-la-Lys;* ⊕ *daily; free entry*) This is the only cemetery on the Western Front dedicated exclusively to Australian soldiers.

Created after the Armistice, the cemetery – covered with immaculate lawns – marks the two mass graves of 410 Australian soldiers who died in the attack at Fromelles, which claimed the lives of more than 5,500 Australians and 1,500 British fighters on 19–20 July 1916. Though their bodies were found on the battlefield, none could be identified, so they were recorded on the memorial along with names of the other 1,208 Australian soldiers with no known grave.

Many have since been named, thanks in larger part to the excavation of the Pheasant Wood mass grave site in 2009 (see below). Visit w vwma.org.au/explore/cemeteries/18 for further information, especially for Australian visitors.

Pheasant Wood Military Cemetery (*Rue de la Basse Ville, opposite the St Jean-Baptiste Church;* ⊕ *daily; free entry*) Pheasant Wood cemetery, dedicated in 2010, is the newest Commonwealth War Graves Commission cemetery on the Western Front. It was built specifically to accommodate the remains of soldiers exhumed from mass graves that had lain undetected in the nearby Pheasant Wood for 92 years.

That they were located at all was mainly due to extensive research by Lambis Eglezos, a retired Greek-born school teacher from Melbourne. His findings were based initially on German archives passed on by local historian Jean-Marie Bailleul. In 2007 and 2008, Lambis, working with British historian Peter Barton, had sufficient evidence to suggest that between 225 and 400 Australian and British soldiers were buried in eight burial pits. Identification of the bodies has been complicated by the need for a female descendant to establish a familial match. Given most of the victims were young single men, with no descendants, this proved to be more difficult than anticipated.

Most of the Pheasant Wood soldiers were killed behind German lines. Many were from the Australian 8th Brigade who had penetrated furthest into the German position at Fromelles. However, their success was short-lived, having found themselves in a classic tactical conundrum of over extending and getting cut off. While some fought their way back to friendly lines, many were either killed or captured.

On 19 July 2010, the then Prince Charles joined scores of relatives to mark its dedication and also the burial, with full military honours, of the 250th soldier discovered and named. The coffin was taken there by a military wagon drawn by horses from the King's Troop Royal Artillery.

Battle of Fromelles Museum (*Rue de la Basse Ville;* ☏ *03 59 61 15 14;* w *musee-bataille-fromelles.fr;* ⏱ *09.30–17.30 Wed–Mon; adults/concessions €5/3, under 8s, disabled, holders of C'ART or City Pass free*) Opened on 18 July 2014 and designed by architect David Serero, this must-see octagonal building in the shape of a German blockhouse is half buried to establish a contemporary link between sky and earth. Among the artefacts is a faded photo of Adolf Hitler – then a 27-year-old corporal rumoured to have been among the German ranks. The permanent exhibition uses faithful reconstructions, period objects and documents, as well as digital resources, to explain the battle's sequence of events, together with the living conditions suffered by the troops. An 'Our Stories' collection sheds fresh light on those already identified in the mass graves of Pheasant Wood (see opposite). Historical research carried out by museum staff means that more details are still being discovered about those who died.

Australian Memorial Park Located 200m from the VC Corner Memorial (see opposite), this park is best known for *Cobbers* – a sculpture by Australian Peter Corlett, which portrays Sergeant, later Second Lieutenant, Simon Fraser, a 38-year-old farmer from Victoria, rescuing a 60th Battalion comrade from No Man's Land.

The dedication panel at the foot of the sculpture provides a quote from him written on 31 July 1916 '…for the next three days we did great work in getting in the wounded from the front and I must say (the Germans) treated us very fairly… we must have brought in over 250 men by our company alone'.

Fraser, who enlisted in July 1915, had already served for nine years as a Sergeant and Acting Colour Sergeant with the Victorian Mounted Rifles and was cited for his distinguished and gallant services and devotion to duty in the Field by Sir Douglas Haig in his 13 November 1916 dispatch.

From 30 March 1917, he was promoted to the rank of Second Lieutenant while at the AIF depot in Tadworth on Salisbury Plain, from where he joined the 58th Battalion in France. He was killed in action only a few days later during the attack on Bullecourt, east of Arras.

Walk An 8.5km signposted walk follows the footsteps of the Allied soldiers. Departing from Fromelles Church, the 2½-hour circuit takes a comprehensive look at ten major sites, with picnic areas and amenities along the way. Pick up a copy of the highly detailed and well-illustrated booklet from any local tourist office.

Cobbers statue, Australian Memorial Park (SS)

The legendary rescue of a rusting World War I British tank called 'Deborah' has taken two major twists since being dug from the battlefield mud around the village of **Flesquières** (11km from Cambrai off the E19/A2) on 5 November 1998. Not only is she now the centre-piece of the **Cambrai Tank 1917 museum** (*16 Rue de Calvaire;* w *tourisme-cambresis.fr;* ⊕ *mid-Jun–mid-Sep 13.45–17.30 daily, otherwise 14.00–17.30 Wed, Sat & Sun; €6*) – which was appropriately opened on 26 November 2017, the centenary of the Battle of Cambrai – but fresh facts have emerged following the persistence of local historian Philippe Gorcynski in tracking down the buried tank's original location.

It involved six years of research and collaboration between British and German archives, the Tank Museum, Bovington and the Imperial War Museum in London. Their findings were largely based on an account by a villager, Madame Bouleux, then a teenager, who claimed to have seen Russian prisoners being ordered by the Germans to push a tank into an enormous hole. Which later begged the question: how could a whole tank be moved 900 yards between where it was destroyed and found?

Philippe now has proof it was actually buried by the British as a shelter and that Deborah was pulled by other tanks to the hole previously dug by German soldiers prior to the Battle of Cambrai.

Up until 2017, Deborah was known simply as D51 – one of only seven Mark IV tanks that survived from a production run of over 1,200. She was put out of action by a field gun while leaving the ferocious fighting in Flesquières – with four of the eight-man crew being killed in the process. The tank's commander, Second Lieutenant Frank Heap, was awarded the Military Cross, the citation referring to how 'he collected the remainder of his crew and conducted them in good order back to our own lines in spite of heavy machine gun and snipers fire'.

Deborah was not discovered until the next day. The four deceased crewmen were buried next to the tank and later re-interred at Hill British Cemetery. The village was not retaken by the Germans until March 1918. Prior to that, the wrecked tank remained in British hands, before being abandoned.

However, the story does not end there. Second Lieutenant Heap's citation referred to four killed servicemen and, for a long time, four headstones, lying side-by-side, showed the names of Gunner J Cheverton, Gunner W Galway, Gunner

CAMBRAI

The areas around Cambrai were the location of two battles: the First Battle of Cambrai (20 November–3 December 1917), which involved the first successful use of tanks; and the Second Battle of Cambrai (8–10 October 1918).

GETTING THERE AND AWAY From Calais **by car**, follow the A26/E15 southeast, past Arras (*146km; approx 1hr 35mins*). Toll charge €11.10 each way. If arriving at Lille Europe via Eurostar, change to Lille Flandres for the regular direct **trains** to Cambrai, which can take up to an hour.

TOURIST INFORMATION

Cambrai Tourist Office   48 Rue Henri de Lubac; ☎ 03 27 78 36 15; w tourisme-cambresis. fr; ⊕ 09.30–12.30 & 14.00–18.00 Mon–Sat, 14.30–17.30 Sun (closed Sun Nov–Mar)

F W Tipping and Private W G Robinson – but there was a complication. A fifth, belonging to Lance Corporal George Charles Foot of the 4th Battalion Tank Corps, who was also killed on the same day, confusingly stood nearby.

Though it was common for casualties to be buried hastily on the battlefield and then exhumed for reburial in post-war military cemeteries, the Commonwealth War Graves Commission records showed that Lance Corporal Foot and gunners Cheverton, Galway and Tipping were originally buried together – with Private Robinson initially interred elsewhere. It was therefore concluded that the four who died in 'Mr Heap's bus' were in fact Foot, Cheverton, Galway and Tipping. Robinson must have been killed elsewhere in the village in another tank. Or so it seemed until the Association du Tank de Flesquières (w *tank-cambrai.com/en*) received an extraordinarily poignant hand-written letter from the nephew of George Foot, written by Frank Heap to George's father, saying: 'I am having a bitter evening now, as four more of my men have also gone, all finer fellows than I shall ever be'. This indicated that despite everything believed previously, the death toll in Deborah was *five* not four. Only two men must have survived with their commander. Private Robinson's name has since been added to the casualty list. Will more revelations follow? You never know with Deborah...

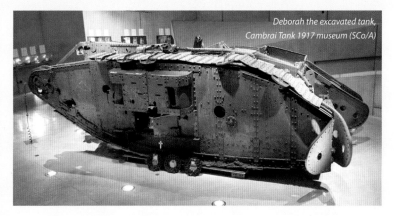

Deborah the excavated tank, Cambrai Tank 1917 museum (SCo/A)

WHAT TO SEE AND DO

Cambrai Battlefield As the tank museum (see box, above) shows, although this battlefield was among the least visited, it was the scene of some of the bloodiest fighting of the war, which ended in a virtual stalemate. It also proved groundbreaking in the Allies' use of massed tanks and aircraft. This tactical innovation, intensively studied by the Germans, evolved into the blitzkrieg methods of the German Army in World War II. It also led to an end to the deadlock, which had paralysed the war since 1914.

British tanks were the most spectacular of these innovations (see box, opposite), used successfully on a large scale for the first time despite earlier disasters, such as their use at the Battle of the Somme in 1916 (see box, page 80). On 20 November 1917, the attack began along a 10km-wide front, with the Tank Corps providing 324 tanks, leading six infantry divisions. The bombardment took the Germans by surprise and, helped by shellfire, the tanks quickly reached the enemy trenches.

A British tank en route to the Battle of Cambrai (SS)

Some 8,000 German prisoners were taken on the first day alone. By the evening, the British vanguard had gained 9km and was closing in.

But then it went badly wrong. Cavalry reinforcements, who were supposed to exploit the German disarray, were placed too far behind the lines. It took 15 hours to cover the final highly congested 5km to the Front.

The Germans rapidly reorganised and the push to Cambrai by British and Canadian forces was thwarted; by 29 November the enemy had sufficient reserves to counterattack. On 3 December, Haig gave orders to withdraw 'with the least possible delay.' All the ground gained in the initial stages had to be abandoned with high losses on both sides: 44,000 killed, wounded and lost in action on the Allied side and about 50,000 on the German side. But the trench stalemate had been broken for the first time since 1914, setting in motion the end of the war in 1918.

ORS

Despite its diminutive size, Ors played an important role in the war.

GETTING THERE AND AWAY From Calais **by car**, follow the A26/E15 southeast to Cambrai, then take the D643 to Ors (*182km; approx 2hrs 5mins*). Ors does have a station, but **trains** are very infrequent.

TOURIST INFORMATION Ors doesn't have a tourist office; the nearest is 7.5km away in **Le Cateau-Cambrésis** (*24 Pl du Général de Gaulle;* ✆ *03 27 84 10 94;* w *tourisme-lecateau.fr;* ⏰ *09.30–12.30 & 14.00–18.00 Mon–Sat, except Tue, Sun & public holidays*).

WHAT TO SEE AND DO
Wilfred Owen Memorial (*La Maison Forestière, Route Départementale 959;* ✆ *03 27 84 54 83;* w *wilfredowen.org.uk/the-foresters-house;* ⏰ *from Apr 14.00–18.00 Wed–Fri, 10.00–13.00 Sat, 15.00–18.00 1st Sun of each month; closed in winter; free entry*)

Originally intrigued by English visitors asking after Wilfred Owen, Jacky Duminy, the Mayor of Ors, commissioned Turner Prize-nominee Simon Patterson to create this memorial to the great poet in 1991. Since then the memorial has attracted thousands of visitors drawn to discover the man Dylan Thomas called 'a poet of all times, all places, and all wars'. It's a startling, almost surreal, white snail-shell-shaped structure with a ramp leading to an airy space lit from above. On to its walls, etched in a skin of glass, is Wilfred Owen's 'Dulce et Decorum Est' – his best-known poem that was published posthumously in 1920. As the lights dim, the voice of actor Kenneth Branagh recites 12 of Owen's poems, with silences in between. The performance lasts an hour.

Anyone visiting six years ago would have ended their visit with a walk into the dark, dank cellar in the Forester's House (*La Maison Forestière;* 03 66 32 01 83; w *wilfredowen.org.uk;* school term time *09.30–12.30 & 14.00–17.30 Wed, Sat & Sun, school holidays 09.30–12.30 & 14.00–17.30 daily*) where Owen and 29 others slept on his last night alive, writing to his mother that 'there is no danger down here'. Now, thanks to Dominic Hibberd, Owen's biographer, the house forms part of a new literary shrine to the poet.

The house was empty and semi-dilapidated when Hibberd, then working on his book *Wilfred Owen: The Last Year,* uncovered its true significance. Today, however, the Forester's House is a family-friendly centre that's part of the main Owen memorial, providing tourist information, a shop and cycle rental. Regarded as neither museum nor memorial, the house is more a place of calm conducive to reflection, contemplation and poetry. Poems are projected on the white walls of the house, with artists in residence entertaining audiences passionate about war poems as well as contemporary architecture. Its patron is the Oscar-winning actor Daniel Day-Lewis.

WILFRED OWEN

On 31 October 1918, in a forest close to the tiny village of Ors (7km from Cateau-Cambrésis off the D643 on the D959), one of Britain's greatest wartime poets, Wilfred Owen, scribbled his final letter to his mother by candlelight. Just days later, on 4 November, he was killed in a hail of machine-gun fire beside the Sambre-Oise Canal, a week before Armistice Day. He was just 25 years old.

Owen, who had joined the Manchester Regiment as a private in his early 20s, was gassed during the Battle of the Somme and spent 28 hours holed up with the dismembered body of a fellow officer. When his nerves understandably snapped, doctors declared him unfit to command and he returned to the UK in June 1917 and spent a long spell in hospital near Edinburgh. During this time he collaborated with the celebrated anti-war poet Siegfried Sassoon producing such works of genius as *Anthem for Doomed Youth, Disabled* and *Exposure*. He returned to the Front in late August 1918. Owen is buried in the back corner of Ors Communal Cemetery. His tomb is third from the left in a line of 22 pristine white headstones.

(WO)

New Zealand Memorial, Le Quesnoy (C/W)

LE QUESNOY

Part of the green Avesnois region, Le Quesnoy (pronounced 'kenwaw') provided a break from the horrors of the trenches and the Germans happily held on to Le Nord region's best-protected walled town until a week before the Armistice, when it was reclaimed by a band of brave Kiwis.

GETTING THERE AND AWAY From Calais **by car**, follow the E40/A16 towards Dunkerque, branch on to the A25/E42 towards Lille/Rijsel. South of Lille, take the A23 to Valenciennes, then follow the A2, then the D649, then branch on to the D934 south to Le Quesnoy (*175km; approx 1hr 50mins*). Regular weekday **rail** services depart from Lille Flandres (*1hr*).

TOURIST INFORMATION
Le Quesnoy Tourist Office 1 Rue du Maréchal Joffre; ☏ 03 27 20 54 70; w tourisme-lequesnoy. com; ⏰ 09.00–12.30 & 14.00–17.00 Mon–Fri, 10.00–12.30 & 15.00–18.00 Sat–Sun & public holidays. See also w nzhistory.govt.nz/war/le-quesnoy/new-zealand-and-le-quesnoy.

WHAT TO SEE AND DO
New Zealand Memorial (*Rue Jeanne d'Arc, or L'Av des Néo-Zélandais*) A week before the November 1918 Armistice, a group of New Zealand soldiers liberated Le Quesnoy in an act worthy of James Bond himself. It would be New Zealand's last major action of the war.

At 05.30 on 4 November, under heavy mortar fire and smoke from burning oil drums, a few soldiers from the Fourth Battalion Third Rifle Brigade attempted to scale the town's ramparts by propping up a ladder, but this proved too short, so they used a narrow stone wall to cross the surrounding moat instead.

At the same time, Captain Napier, a mortar expert, shelled the top of the walls. By 16.00, bewildered German soldiers faced an onslaught by rampart-scaling Kiwis.

After strong resistance, during which the New Zealand Division suffered 400 casualties, with 93 killed in action, the 1,500 Germans surrendered. Sixty-five of the New Zealanders who died here are buried in Le Quesnoy. Pinned to the ramparts is a carved relief panel depicting the dramatic events, an angel watching over the soldiers and a silver fern – the Kiwi national emblem.

None of the 55,000 French residents at the time lost their lives and their gratitude remains as strong as ever: *Teko Teko* – the town's Maori giant, given to the town in 1972 by the New Zealand Rifle Brigade – shares pride of place with Pierre Bimberlot, Le Quesnoy's wicker giant.

New Zealand Liberation Museum (*18 Rue Achille Carlier;* w *nzliberationmuseum. com;* ⊕ *1 Apr–31 Oct 10.30–18.00 Wed–Sun, 1 Nov–31 Mar 09.30–17.00 Wed–Sun, closed 24 Dec–31 Jan; adult/60+/6–18/under 6s €15/12/8/free*) A brand new museum scheduled to open in October 2023, explaining the heroic 1918 liberation of Le Quesnoy after four years of German occupation using artworks, soundscapes, projections and emotive storytelling. Its Maori name is Te Arawhata, meaning 'ladder' – a reference to the tool used to scale the walled town surreptitiously instead of using gunfire. Don't miss it.

Beaudignies Also maintaining a strong affinity with New Zealand is the nearby village of Beaudignies, which renamed its main square Place du Colonel Blyth in honour of LM (Curly) Blyth, a young subaltern in the 3rd New Zealand (Rifle) Brigade, in 2000.

Along with other surviving veterans of the Western Front, Blyth was created a Chevalier de la Légion d'Honneur in 1998 and a Member of the New Zealand Order of Merit three years later 'for services to war veterans and the community'. At the time of his death on 10 October 2001, at the age of 105, Lieutenant-Colonel Blyth was one of the last two remaining veterans of the New Zealand Expeditionary Force.

MAUBEUGE/FEIGNIES

Despite being heavily fortified, this major iron and steel district, situated on the Sambre River, was heavily hammered in both World War I and II – it still shows.

GETTING THERE AND AWAY From Calais **by car**, follow the E40/A16 towards Dunkerque, branch on to the A25/E42 towards Lille/Rijsel. South of Lille, take the A23 to Valenciennes, then follow the D649 east past Bavay to Maubeuge (*194km; approx 2hrs*). Regular **rail** services depart from Valenciennes (*40mins*) and from Lille (*1hr 20mins*).

TOURIST INFORMATION

Maubeuge Tourist Office Porte de Mons, Pl Vauban; ☎ 03 27 62 11 93; w uk.maubeuge-tourisme.com; ⊕ Jul–Sep 09.00–12.30 & 13.30– 18.00 Mon–Fri, 09.00–12.30 & 13.30–17.00 Sat, 09.30–13.30 Sun; Oct–Jun 09.00–12.30 & 13.30–17.00 Mon–Sat

WHAT TO SEE AND DO

Fort de Leveau (*Rue de Mairieux, Feignies;* ☎ 03 27 62 37 07; w *fortdeleveau.fr;* ⊕ *15 Feb–31 Mar & Nov 13.00–17.00 Mon–Fri, 1 Apr–31 Oct 13.00–17.00 Mon–Fri, 14.30–18.00 last 2 Sun of the month; guided tours start at 15.00; closed holidays except 11 Nov 14.30–18.00; adult/10–16/under 10s €5/2/free*) One of 11 fortified positions surrounding the town of **Maubeuge** – just 9km from the Belgian border

Fort de Leveau (ASFL)

– Leveau Fort in Feignies stood at a key intersection of the Brussels–Liège railway line to Paris. Early in World War I the German Army, who were eager to press on to the French capital for a quick victory over France, had it in their sights. They were hindered by the Allied forces of France, Belgium and Britain, but after a two-week siege between 27 August and 7 September 1914 – the longest of its kind in World War I – Leveau Fort's defenders were forced to surrender when the 60,000-strong German troops flattened the outer fortifications with shells fired from long-range German guns. Nevertheless, Allied forces had prevented a hefty number of German soldiers from taking part in the First Battle of the Marne (see box, page 104), which began on 5 September. In 1998, excavations recovered the remains of nine soldiers killed in the 1914 siege and they were re-interred at the French–German Assevent Cemetery at Maubeuge.

A fixed bridge and drawbridge, destroyed by the shelling, was rebuilt to commemorate the siege and this was inaugurated on 6 September 2014. Further improvements to the museum were carried out in 2017, with high-tech exhibits that delve into the history of French forts, alongside life as a Great War soldier.

Pas-de-Calais: Arras, Lens and the Ports

ARRAS

Arras was central to some of the fiercest fighting of World War I and reduced to ruins in the conflict. Not that you would notice now, such was the brilliance in rebuilding from the rubble replicas of the glorious 17th- and 18th-century gabled buildings around the cobbled twin squares. Today, the capital of Pas-de-Calais is positively cosmopolitan and an ideal centre for exploring the battlefields, with interest generated by five special events that led to it becoming 'one of the martyred cities of France': see w arras1418.com for full details.

GETTING THERE AND AWAY Travelling **by car** from the Calais ferry, follow the A26/E15 south (*112km; approx 1hr*). For **trains** from Gare Lille Europe, change platforms for the fast TGV service to Arras (*30mins*); there are also regular trains from Gare Lille Flandres (*1hr*).

TOURIST INFORMATION Arras Tourist Office trains and works with a number of local guides and can arrange **battlefield tours** on your behalf. Alternatively, you could contact the Guild of Battlefield Guides for further information (w *gbg-international.com*).

Arras Tourist Office Town Hall, Pl des Héros; 03 21 51 26 95; w explorearras.com; ⏰ mid-Sep–31 Mar 10.00–noon & 14.00–18.00 Mon, 09.00–noon & 14.00–18.00 Tue–Sat, 10.00–12.30 & 14.30–18.30 Sun; 1 Apr–mid-Sep 09.00–18.30 Mon–Sat, 10.00–13.00 & 14.30–18.30 Sun. Free maps & accommodation information. See website for city passes & guided tours featuring World War I sites (some tickets available in advance).

WHAT TO SEE AND DO
Wellington Tunnels (Carrière Wellington) (*Rue Arthur Delétoile;* 03 21 51 26 95; w *carrierewellington.com;* ⏰ *10.00–12.30 & 13.30–18.00 daily; adult/child €7.20/3.50; audio-guide detour available & private bilingual tours upon request, but check with tourist office*) From their discovery in 1990, these connecting tunnels and underground quarries – some dating back to Roman times – have drawn a worldwide audience earning them a top place in the town's tourist attractions.

It was through here and similar tunnels that some 24,000 soldiers – the equivalent of the population of Arras just before the outbreak of war – emerged, blinking in the early morning sleet of Easter Monday, 9 April 1917, to fight an unsuspecting enemy in the Battle of Arras (see box, page 62).

In 1917, Arras was under Allied control, but the town had been taking a pasting since October 1914. A tantalising salient – the military term for a pocket of ground that juts into enemy territory – had developed and Field Marshal Douglas Haig (see box, page 76) and his French counterpart needed to devise a way to breach the German line. Arras, they decided, would be used in a diversionary offensive, drawing in enemy reserves for several days before the French launched a large-scale bid to break the enemy stranglehold on the Chemin des Dames ridge in the Champagne region (page 92).

There was one big snag: how could the Allies concentrate a large number of troops near the Front Line without arousing suspicion? Fearful of the slaughter experienced in the battles of Verdun and the Somme, the commanders suggested a daring solution: to create a vast network of tunnels enabling troops to emerge directly in front of the German line rather than facing the deadly machine-gun fire of No Man's Land.

So at 05.30 on 9 April 1917, an enormous explosion was the signal for more than 24,000 men to surge from their underground hiding places to appear directly in front of enemy lines. There was no time for the Germans to raise the alarm. Some were still found in their pyjamas in a nearby village.

Though the first few days were a tactical success, with the Germans forced to fall back on their second line of defence, it proved a costly offensive. Heavy reinforcements led to vigorous counterattacks and a series of bloody battles, but the Allies were able to push the combat zone back some 10km and relieve the pressure on Arras. More than 150,000 British casualties were reported between April and May 1917; total losses for the Germans are presumed to have been around the same. While the ground advancements were impressive considering the Western Front stalemate, the high losses and ultimate failure of the Allied offensive overshadowed the gains.

The battle will perhaps be best remembered for the taking of **Vimy Ridge**, when four Canadian Divisions of the British Army separately set out on the same day to conquer the 145m-high ridge – dubbed 'The Pimple' – whose position allowed the Germans to fire freely at Allied forces. Heavily fortified, with several lines of trenches punctuated with concrete shelters, the ridge had proved impenetrable – all previous attempts to take the hilltop fortress had failed.

However, in the months leading up to the attack, the Canadians had dug a 10km network of tunnels that ran to the Front. Within 30 minutes of the attack, their path cleared by cannon fire and tanks, the Canadian Divisions had overrun part of the German Front Line and, within an hour, parts of the second too.

By the middle of the afternoon, despite heavy losses inflicted during the initial wave, they controlled most of the ridge. The next day they took possession of Hill 145, where the famous memorial now stands. Two days later, the whole ridge was under Allied control and the Germans had been forced back into the surrounding coal basin. The Canadians took 3,400 prisoners in three days along a 14km stretch. It was an outright victory, but losses were high: between 9 and 14 April, 10,600 men were either killed or wounded.

Housed in one of the original medieval subterranean chalk quarries, the two interconnecting labyrinths were created by 500 New Zealanders, predominantly Maori coal and gold miners, aided by 'bantams' – Yorkshire miners who didn't meet the Army's minimum-height requirement of five feet three inches. But amid the post-war chaos and the wish to forget, they lay forgotten until 1990 when Alain Jacques, in charge of Arras's archaeology department, decided to investigate the *boves* (caves) in which a few locals sheltered during World War II.

Along with Jean-Marie Prestaux, the enthusiastic former director of tourism, Jacques worked out that one quarry, known as Wellington – one of a number named after the Kiwi tunnellers and home to the Suffolk Regiment – lay under a former council-owned campsite, allowing for reconstruction to take place. The others had either collapsed, were unsafe, or in some cases, had houses built over them.

The €4 million visitor attraction offers a 75-minute portrayal of the underground privations leading up to the fateful spring offensive. After a short introduction, visitors, accompanied by a bilingual expert and equipped with audio-guides, take a glass-walled lift 20m down to a compelling World War I world, where a film along with drawings, fading photos and graffiti bring a terrifying touch of authenticity.

AROUND ARRAS

BEAURAINS
The CWGC Visitor Centre (*7 Rue Angèle Richard, 62217 Beaurains;* \ *01 21 52 75;* w *cwgc.org/visit-us/the-cwgc-experience;* ◷ *Mar–Nov 09.00–16.00 Mon–Fri; free entry & audio guide*) Opened by Princess Anne in 2019, the CWGC Experience is 'emphatically not a museum' but instead showcases how the Commonwealth War Grave Commission's teams of experts tend to 23,000 locations in more than 150 countries. This encompasses everything from mowing the equivalent of 1,000 football pitches to exhuming around 40 bodies annually. The latter often means sifting through a mix of artefacts – such as a fraying boot, helmet, or a spoon with

Gravestones being made at the CWGC Visitor Centre (PCT)

CHURCHES MARK SCOTS' HIGH DEATH TOLL

In 2017, church services on both sides of the Channel marked the 100th anniversary of the Battle of Arras, during which 18,000 Scottish soldiers died. Though Scottish battalions played a major role at Loos (see box, page 70) and on the Somme, 44 in all took part in this crucial set-piece of World War I, with one-third of the 159,000 casualties being Scottish.

a possible tell-tale army number on it – to try and identify some of the 217,000 World War I soldiers killed in France with no known grave. It can be dangerous work with still-unexploded grenades or mustard bombs posing a risk. Their task is humbling.

SAINT-LAURENT-BLANGY

Bailleul Road East Cemetery (*Follow D919 from Laurent-Blangy toward Bailleul-sire-Berthoult for 2.5km; ⊕ daily; free entry*) Work on the rubble-wall-encircled cemetery was begun by the 34th Division in April 1917 and continued by fighting units until the following November with further plots added in August 1918. It consolidated a series of isolated graves from around Arras, including 69 British soldiers from the **Northumberland Cemetery** in Fampoux and **Lagnicourt**.

German Military Cemetery (*Chemin de Bailleul; ⊕ daily; free entry*) Black crosses mark the graves of 7,069 German soldiers who died during World War I, while a mass grave contains the remains of 24,870 soldiers, over half of whom were never identified. When the remains of a further 4,283 soldiers were moved from the German section of Comines Cemetery near Lille, it became the second-largest German cemetery in France (after La Maison Blanche; see page 68) – home to over 36,000 souls.

MONCHY-LE-PREUX

Newfoundland Memorial (*Rue de Chaussy; ⊕ daily; free entry*) Lying 9km east of Arras, the village of Monchy-le-Preux crowns a conical hill about 1km north of the main Arras–Cambrai road. Standing atop a German post in the centre of town, a bronze statue of a caribou is one of five (there's another in Beaumont-Hamel; page 85) erected in honour of the Newfoundland soldiers who took part in World War I – the Newfoundland Regiment (the Royal Newfoundland Regiment from 28 September 1917) was one of seven battalions with Scottish heritage.

MONT-SAINT-ÉLOI

Ruined towers and lookout (*Rue de la Mairie;* ⏺ *daily; free entry*) An abbey was established here in the 7th century but pillaged for its stone during the Revolution. When World War I broke out, all that remained of the abbey were the twin towers of the west wall. Nevertheless, these towers provided an invaluable lookout point for the French, who could see the German lines set up on Vimy Ridge and Lorette Spur. Heavy shelling during the war shortened the towers by about 10m and the ruins today are a living monument to the destruction and devastation caused by war.

VIMY Occupation of Vimy Ridge gave either side a particularly good view of the locality – especially from Hill 145, which was the highest point in the whole area. This made it a prize possession and, from the Allies' point of view, the German occupation of the ridge was a major threat to any advance in the Somme region in 1917. Therefore, the decision was taken to hand the task of reclaiming it to the Canadians.

Canadian National Vimy Memorial (*Route départementale 55; follow signs from the village of Vimy off the N17 reached via junction 7 on the E15/A26; the memorial & other sites are well signposted;* ⏺ *year round; free entry*) It is difficult not to be deeply affected by the Vimy Memorial, which overlooks the Douai Plain from the highest point of Vimy Ridge, about 10km north of Arras. The white twin-columned monolith

Canadian National Vimy Memorial (WM/S)

stands alone in open country slightly north of the 240-acre Canadian Memorial Park (see below) of which it forms a part.

The memorial, work on which began in 1925, commemorates not just the 1917 Easter Sunday Battle of Vimy Ridge, but the 66,000 Canadians killed overall in World War I, of whom 11,285 have no known graves.

Each column stands 45m high. One bears a maple leaf; the other a fleur-de-lis symbolising the sacrifice of both Canada and France. The columns and the sculpted figures (created by Canadian artists) together contain almost 6,000 tons of limestone brought from an abandoned Roman quarry on the Adriatic Sea (in present-day Croatia). The largest piece, carved from a 30-ton block, shows a grieving figure of a woman representing Canada in mourning. It took 11 years and US$1.5 million to build and rests on a bed of 11,000 tons of concrete, reinforced with hundreds of tons of steel. The work of Toronto sculptor and designer Walter Seymour Allward, it was inspired, he said, from a dream and was unveiled on 26 July 1936 by King Edward VIII.

Canadian Memorial Park

This area of parkland on the territory of the commune of Givenchy-en-Gohelle was granted to Canada by the French in 1922. Here, among 11,285 Canadian trees and shrubs – reflecting the number 'missing' in war – families stroll over grass-covered shell holes and mine craters.

Others play games or jog along gravel paths that run alongside a huge crater, one of 14 created when hidden Allied mines were exploded on Easter Monday, 9 April 1917, during the Battle of Arras (see box, page 62).

There were more than a dozen large tunnels, known as subways, dug by the 172nd Tunnelling Company of the British Royal Engineers with the help of the 7th Canadian Infantry Brigade. These were used for the safe passage of around 950 Canadian soldiers as they moved to the Front. The best surviving tunnel is the Grange Subway, with roughly 250m remaining of the original 1,230m.

The Ring of Remembrance at Notre-Dame de Lorette French National War Cemetery (T/S)

A huge number of artillery shells were also fired into the area and remain dangerous to this day with red-zone areas fenced off to visitors, though the sheep graze happily enough in them. Also notice that in places the German and Allied positions are only 25m apart.

Entry to the Memorial Park site is free of charge, though parts of the site may be closed to the public in severe weather. Replacing the original in 2017, the now high-tech **Vimy Visitor Education Centre** (*03 21 50 68 68; Oct 1–Mar 31 11.00–17.00 Mon, 09.00–17.00 Tue–Sun, closed mid-Dec to beginning of Feb; free entry*) is a short, well-signposted drive from the memorial, or a 10-minute walk. It helps visitors connect with the surrounding landscape and houses the poignant 'We Will Remember' exhibition featuring a collection of faded photos and videos. Artefacts on display include wooden tools used by Allward, an original cross from the Battle of Vimy Ridge with the names of 57 members of the 15th Battalion (48th Highlanders of Canada) who fell during the battle, and a huge, haunting, colourised photograph of exhausted soldiers returning from the Battle of the Somme. Thirty-minute **guided tours of the preserved trench and tunnel system** take place every 30 minutes from the visitor centre during opening hours. Expect uneven terrain, enclosed spaces and a descent of up to 10m underground. Children under the age of 12 must be accompanied by an adult to take part; sadly both the trench and tunnel are unsuitable for wheelchair users.

ABLAIN-SAINT-NAZAIRE

Notre-Dame de Lorette French National War Cemetery (*Ablain-Saint-Nazaire, signposted off the D937 between Arras & Béthune; 08.00–18.30; free entry*) France's largest military cemetery contains 39,985 burials with an additional number of French and other nationalities from World War II. A plot devoted to Muslim soldiers can be found at the western end of the cemetery.

Situated on a plateau, it has a remarkable view of the eastern part of the Gohelle Plain dominated by twin slag heaps, known as 11/19, and the Artois hills in the west. Look out for the Lantern Tower, the beacon of which revolves five times each minute after darkness falls. Volunteer Honour Guards stand daily at the ossuary between Palm Sunday and Remembrance Day on 11 November. Facing it is **The Ring of Remembrance**. With a radius of more than 345m – the length of almost four football pitches – and inspired by Parisian architect Philippe Prost, the ring names 579,606 soldiers from 40 different nationalities in alphabetical order with no reference to rank or religion. These are recorded on 500 metal panels, each 3m high. The first is that of a Nepalese sailor, the last that of a German soldier. The 500th panel remains blank so that any newly discovered names can be inscribed.

SOUCHEZ

14–18 Notre-Dame-de-Lorette Memorial History Centre (*102 Rue Pasteur; 03 21 74 83 85; w memorial1418.com; 1 Apr–11 Nov 10.00–13.00 & 14.00–18.00 Wed–Fri, 11.00–13.00 & 14.00–18.00 Sat & Sun, 12 Nov–31 Mar 13.00–17.00 Wed–Sun; free except for special events, youth booklet for €3, audio guide €3*) Formerly known as the Lens 14–18 War and Peace Centre, this exhibition space is located in the middle of the former battlefields and was designed by French architect Pierre-Louis Faloci to resemble the sober black concrete cubes of the World War I blockhouses. The interior, which allows for shafts of light from the surrounding fields, features a permanent exhibition that combines an outstanding collection of maps illustrating different offensives, archive film footage and photographs, some almost life size.

Cabaret-Rouge British Cemetery (SS)

An image of soldiers blinded by poison gas walking in single file, all with bandaged eyes, is one of the most enduring.

Musée Vivant 14/18 (*Colline de Notre-Dame-de-Lorette, behind the cemetery*) Just west of the 14–18 Memorial Centre and featuring more than 3,000 items, the museum traces life in the French Army through equipment, uniforms, documents and photographs. Look out for the diorama presenting rare 3D 1914–18 images. Outside, a battlefield area is dedicated to trenches – redug in their original locations – along with a selection of artillery pieces, machine guns, shells and barbed wire. A small shop sells souvenirs, books and postcards. Discounted rates for visits to both museums are available.

Cabaret-Rouge British Cemetery (*1.5km south of Souchez on the west side of the D937 Arras–Béthune road*) Named after the red-brick Cabaret Rouge café located nearby, the cemetery served as one of a small number of 'open cemeteries' where the remains of fallen servicemen, newly discovered in the region, were buried. Today, the cemetery contains over 7,650 burials from World War I – over half of which remain unidentified. They include those of British, Irish, Australian, New Zealand, Indian and South African soldiers; it is also the final resting place for over 70 officers of the Royal Flying Corps and Royal Air Force.

Cabaret-Rouge also has a particularly close connection to the Canadian Infantry, with hundreds of those killed at Vimy Ridge buried here. In May 2000, the remains of an unknown Canadian soldier were taken from this cemetery and buried in a special tomb at the foot of the National War Memorial in Ottawa, Canada.

In anticipation of the World War I centenary, major renovation works started in May 2013, with headstones replaced and borders replanted.

NEUVILLE-SAINT-VAAST
La Maison Blanche German War Cemetery (*Route de Béthune, Neuville-Saint-Vaast; 8km off the D973/D55 to Béthune*) This is the largest German war cemetery in France, with a total of 44,843 soldiers buried beneath black crosses each bearing

the names of four individuals. Only 8,040 remain unidentified and these unknown souls are buried in a mass grave. A relief map at the entrance represents the battlefield on which the cemetery was built.

AROUND LENS

LOOS-EN-GOHELLE

Loos British Cemetery (*121 Rue Roger Salengro, 62750 Loos-en-Gohelle;* ⏱ *daily; free entry*) At the time of writing, the total number of burials here is 2,850, of which 2,403 were from the UK, 446 from Canada and one from France. Of these, two thirds are unidentified. Over the last five years, the remains of a substantial number of World War I casualties have been uncovered across northern France, including those recovered from the site of a new hospital being built at Lens, and so the decision was taken to build an extension for the soldiers who have remained missing since the war. The extension began in April 2023 and should open to the public in the autumn of 2024.

Musée Alexandre Villedieu (*1st Flr, Pl de la République;* ☏ *06 60 40 06 22;* e *contact@loos1915.fr;* w *tourisme-lenslievin.fr;* ⏱ *by appointment only*) The by-appointment-only museum provides a comprehensive collection of everyday objects from the battlefield grouped by nationality. It's named after French soldier Alexandre Villedieu, who disappeared on 8 October 1915 but whose remains were found in 1966 along with his personal effects, including his fountain pen with its original ink. His body now rests at the national necropolis of our Lady of Lorette in Ablain-Saint-Nazaire. His pen is on display in a wooden case. Arms, dishes, identification bracelets and assault plans all help complete the collection, gathered through links with the descendants of soldiers from all over the world, especially the UK, Canada and Germany.

Hill 70 Memorial Park (*Rue Louis Faidherbe;* e *hill70mp@gmail.com*) Dedicated to the Canadian Corps that achieved victory at the Battle of Hill 70 in August 1917, the memorial's centrepiece is an obelisk topped by a Sword of Sacrifice. Pace the series of walkways dedicated to the six Victoria Cross awards, as well as plazas dedicated to regiments and soldiers who figured prominently in the battle.

Dud Corner Cemetery (*Route de Béthune, 1km west of Loos;* ⏱ *year-round; free entry*) This cemetery contains the graves of over 2,000 soldiers, of which over half are unidentified – most were killed in the Battle of Loos. At the back stands the semicircular **Loos Memorial** engraved with the names of 20,000 soldiers with no known graves who fell in the Lys River area. The name 'Dud Corner' possibly stems from the number of unexploded enemy shells found following the Armistice.

HAISNES

St Mary's Advanced Dressing Station Cemetery (*Follow the Commonwealth War Graves Commission sign on the D947 Lens to La Bassée Road; the cemetery lies off this on the D39 Hulloch to Vermelles Raod;* ☏ *03 21 25 43 43;* ⏱ *year-round; free entry*) The village of Haisnes-lez-La-Bassé was nearly reached by the 9th (Scottish) and 7th Divisions on the first day of the Battle of Loos. The battlefield clearance cemetery, which lies in farmland, was created after the Armistice; the great majority of the graves are of those killed in action between September and October 1915.

The brutal Battle of Loos (appropriately pronounced 'Loss') was fought between 25 September and 4 November 1915. Like those at Arras and Vimy Ridge, the battle was part of the wider **Artois–Loos Offensive** which, conducted by the British and French, was sometimes known as the Third Battle of Artois. It was launched simultaneously with the main French offensive in Champagne.

Six divisions were committed to the attack, despite Douglas Haig's (see box, page 76) fears over a worrying shortage of shells and exhaustion among his troops. He was even more concerned about the difficult terrain that needed crossing, but his troops far outnumbered the Germans and thus the odds seemed in the Allies' favour. However, having failed to 'soften' enemy trenches with a four-day barrage of 250,000 shells, the British used gas for the first time. The Germans had used it previously in the Battle of Ypres with success, but, in a cruel twist of fate, a change in wind direction blew 140 tonnes of British-deployed chlorine gas back on to British lines. Many soldiers, unable to see through their fogged-up inefficient masks, removed them, which led to seven deaths; another 2,600 had to be withdrawn from the Front Line as a result. The attempted gas attack was an unmitigated disaster.

Meanwhile, the southern end of the attack proved to be a spectacular success. British troops, predominantly Scots, took the village of Loos and Hill 70 under the cover of smokescreens and advanced towards Lens. However, a delay due to lack of munitions and the late arrival of reinforcements allowed the Germans

HARNES

Musée d'Histoire et d'Archéologie (*50 Rue André Deprez;* ☎ *03 21 49 02 29;* ⏱ *14.00–17.00 Mon–Sat; free entry*) This small museum is housed in a late 19th-century mansion and has four rooms devoted to both World Wars, as well as a photographic exhibition showing how the town changed between 1900 and 1950. To get there, buses No 14, 16 and 120 depart Lens regularly (*8km*).

ESCALLES

Moving to France's northern coast, the tranquil landscape that accompanies a drive along the D940 belies the area's centrally important position during the war: the cross-Channel ports were instrumental in keeping Allied supplies flowing as the Germans attempted to close the shipping routes.

GETTING THERE AND AWAY **Bus** No 5 departs from outside Calais theatre and stops in Cap Blanc-Nez in summer, just up the hill from Escalles, and in Sangatte the rest of the year.

WHAT TO SEE AND DO

The Dover Patrol Monument (*Cap Blanc-Nez, D940 north of Escalles, towards Sangatte*) This monument pays tribute to the assortment of Tribal-class destroyer boats, armed trawlers, drifters, yachts and motorboats that joined up with submarines and seaplanes to defend the Strait of Dover from the German Navy throughout World War I. The Patrol kept the waterways navigable and escorted hospital and troop ships, as well as laying and keeping the sea free of mines. Throughout 1917 the Dover Patrol prevented U-boats from leaving German-held to retake Hill 70. Further to the north the British advance was slowed by the formidable defences of the **Hohenzollern Redoubt** – a vast complex of trenches, underground shelters and machine-gun nests. Even so, the British managed to take part of the German line at the Front, but the next day German reinforcements arrived in huge numbers to fill the breaches.

By 28 September, after sporadic fighting for several days, the British general staff gave the order to abandon positions taken the previous day. Another offensive on 13 October again opened with a gas attack but came to a similarly disastrous end in poor weather conditions. In a mere 10 minutes, the 46th Division lost 180 officers and 3,583 men in an attempt to take the Hohenzollern Redoubt. Overall, British casualties at Loos totalled 50,000, including at least 20,000 dead; the Germans lost some 25,000 men. The nature of the fighting also meant that most of the dead were unrecoverable from the battlefield until after the war, three years later. By then, their bodies were unidentifiable, and many cemeteries around Loos contain a high percentage of unknown graves.

The failure at Loos also led to the British Commander in Chief Sir John French being replaced by General Haig in December 1915. The battlefield is situated 5km northwest of the former mining town of Lens, near the village of Loos-en-Gohelle, off the A26 at junction 6 or junction 6.1; follow the signs via the D943.

ports in Belgium and between 22 and 23 April 1918, it raided Zeebrugge and Ostende. A certain Captain E R Evans is remembered for carrying a penguin mascot nailed to the mast of his destroyer – a relic from his days with Captain Scott's ill-fated Antarctic Expedition.

BOULOGNE-SUR-MER

Boulogne-sur-Mer was one of the top three cross-Channel ports that received supplies and troops in World War I. It became an enormous barracks, with public buildings requisitioned to house the wounded evacuated from the Front.

GETTING THERE AND AWAY From Calais **by car**, follow the E402/A16 southwest past Marquise (*34km; approx 30mins*). There are two SNCF **railway stations**: some 15 trains run daily from Gare Calais-Ville to Gare de Boulogne Ville; it's a 15–20-minute walk from Boulogne station to the town centre. Some slow trains stop at Boulogne Tintelleries station.

The Dover Patrol Monument at Cap Blanc-Nez (PCT)

MY SON JACK

(WC)

The short life of John (Jack) Kipling, the son of esteemed British poet Rudyard Kipling, was brought to life by *Harry Potter* star Daniel Radcliffe in the much-acclaimed British TV drama *My Boy Jack*.

Aged just 18, Jack died on 27 September 1915 during the Battle of Loos, but whether the grave bearing his name in St Mary's Advanced Dressing Station Cemetery – a post-war battlefield clearance cemetery (page 69) – is correct has been a matter of much debate. This is mostly due to the rank displayed on the deceased officer's uniform, which was that of a second lieutenant: Jack had been promoted to a full lieutenant. Scholars speculate as to whether his promotion to the higher rank was never gazetted on his arrival in France, hence the error on the gravestone.

There's also confusion regarding the location of the body. Jack Kipling was last seen about a mile and three-quarters southeast of where the cemetery now lies, yet the body listed as his was found about two miles to the southwest. There's even some question as to whether the uniform of the deceased officer, originally described simply as 'a lieutenant of the Irish Guards' was actually that of the Irish Guards.

It was not until June 1992 that the Commonwealth War Graves Commission finally decided that the 'lieutenant' buried had to be Kipling because they could account for all the others who had died during the battle.

Jack's story illustrates the dangers of unbridled patriotism, but reflects the ultimate sacrifice made by so many young soldiers.

TOURIST INFORMATION

Boulogne-sur-Mer Tourist Office 30 Rue de la Lampe; ☏ 03 21 10 88 10; w boulonnaisautop. com; ⏱ 09.30–13.00 & 14.00–18.30 Mon–Sat, 10.00–13.00 & 15.00–18.00 Sun, may change in winter

WHAT TO SEE AND DO

Boulogne Eastern Cemetery (*Rue de Dringhen;* ⏱ *Nov–Feb 08.30–17.00 Mon–Fri, 09.00–17.00 Sat & Sun; Mar–Oct 08.30–18.00 Mon–Fri, 09.00–18.00 Sat & Sun; free entry*) The cemetery contains 5,821 Commonwealth graves (some contain more than one body), of which 5,577 date from World War I and 224 from World War II.

One grave is that of poet **Julian Grenfell** who, in 1914, shocked many by likening the war to 'a big picnic without the objectlessness of a picnic', claiming he had 'never been so well or so happy'. His most famous poem, 'Into Battle', was published on 26 May 1915, a few days after his death in a Boulogne hospital from a shrapnel wound to the head. He was 27 years old.

In spring 1918, with the cemetery at maximum capacity, a new one was opened in the village of Terlincthun near Wimille (north of Boulogne-sur-Mer). After the war, Terlincthun took in graves from isolated plots which could not be adequately maintained. This explains how 200 soldiers from Russia, Poland and the USA, as well as German prisoners of war, lie alongside 4,378 British, Indian and Canadian Commonwealth graves (of which 3,380 are identified).

A further 48 graves belong to members of the Royal Air Force who were killed in September 1918 above the town of **Marquise** – northeast of Boulogne-sur-Mer – during a German bombing raid. It is a stark reminder that World War I opened up a new battleground – the sky – in which the Royal Flying Corps played a major role.

AROUND BOULOGNE-SUR-MER

Wimereux Communal Cemetery (*Rue Jean Moulin;* ⏰ *1 Nov–31 Mar 08.00–17.00 daily, 1 Apr–31 October 8.00–19.00 daily*) Situated 6km north of Boulogne, this cemetery is the site of 2,847 graves of soldiers and nurses who died in the ten British Army field hospitals in the area.

Among them stands the headstone of Lieutenant-Colonel John McCrae, a Canadian doctor and poet who cared for soldiers wounded in the Second Battle of Ypres and who wrote the famous poem 'In Flanders Fields' (see box, page 19).

Saint-Étienne-au-Mont Communal Cemetery (*Rue Edmond Madaré, Saint-Étienne-au-Mont;* ⏰ *daily; free entry*) The rows of white headstones may look like those of a standard Commonwealth cemetery, but in fact they're erected in honour of 160 members of the Chinese Labour Corps (and ten members of the South African Labour Corps). The Labour Corps were made up of civilians who carried out manual tasks, such as felling timber, unloading boat cargo, maintaining railways, etc, freeing up British soldiers for fighting. It must have been incredibly isolating for the Chinese labourers, who didn't speak English, yet by the end of the war there were over 96,000 in British Army service. To get to the cemetery from Boulogne-sur-Mer, take Marineo bus No E or No 1.

Boulogne Eastern Cemetery (W/WC)

ÉTAPLES-SUR-MER

Seen as relatively safe from attack, the protected port of Étaples was selected as the site of a vast training camp thanks to its good rail links to both the northern and southern battlefields. But according to many stationed along the Western Front, Étaples – or 'Eat Apples' as it was nicknamed – was reckoned to be the most detested of all base camps.

In 1917, 100,000 troops were camped here with a variety of hospitals equipped to deal with 22,000 wounded or sick. Conditions at the camp were atrocious, and both recruits and battle-weary veterans were subjected to intensive training

8

Étaples Military Cemetery (PCT)

at the notorious Bull Ring training camp set among the sand dunes. After two weeks, many of the wounded were only too glad to return to the Front with unhealed wounds. There were even clashes between patients and the Military Police.

GETTING THERE AND AWAY From Calais or Boulogne, by **car** follow the E402/A16 for 32km (*35min*) and leave at exit 26 for the D939 (€2.90 toll). By **train**, take the frequent TER service to Étaples-Le Touquet station; it's a 5-minute walk to Étaples town centre. There are also regular **buses** from Boulogne-sur-Mer on line 512 Boulogne–Étaples.

TOURIST INFORMATION
Étaples-sur-Mer Tourist Office La Corderie Bd, Bigot Descelers; 03 21 09 56 94; w tourisme-etaples.com; ⏱ Oct–Mar 10.00–12.30 & 14.00–18.00 Mon–Sat, 14.00–18.00 Sun; Apr–Sep 09.30–13.00 & 14.00–18.00 daily

WHAT TO SEE AND DO
Étaples Military Cemetery (*2km northwest of Étaples off the D940;* ⏱ *year-round; free entry*) Terraced rows of white gravestones provide a grim reminder that, of 11,500 interred here, 10,771 died in or around Étaples during World War I, the earliest dating from May 1915. The tombs recall soldiers from Canada, Australia, New Zealand, South Africa and India as well as 658 German burials. Thirty-five burials remain unidentified.

A further 119 individuals were buried here after World War II – of which 38 remain unidentified – which makes this the largest Commonwealth cemetery in France. Sir Edwin Lutyens designed the towering white-stone arches at the entrance. There is a visitor book where you can leave a message: 'So sad I never met you, Dad' and 'At last I meet you, Granddad' are typical of many. A register shows the location of each grave. Renovations to the terraces are now complete.

MONTREUIL-SUR-MER

Once a port connected to the sea before the Canche River silted up, Montreuil-sur-Mer became the nerve centre of the British Army in March 1916, after it had been initially set up in Saint-Omer in October 1914. Divided into five departments, this vast general headquarters was staffed by a wide range of military personnel and forced this previously sleepy old fortified town into playing a pivotal role in the war.

GETTING THERE AND AWAY By **car**, either join the E402/A16 at Calais and leave at exit 29 for the D901 and the 75km journey, which is toll free, or continue on the E402/A16 and leave at exit 26 for the D939/D901, which might be slightly quicker but is subject to a €2.70 toll each way on the Boulogne stretch of the motorway. If arriving at Calais by **train**, take the frequent TER service from Calais-Ville station to Boulogne-Ville and change to the TER Line 14 (Arras via Étaples and Saint-Pol) for Montreuil-sur-Mer station, which is just a few hundred metres down from the ramparts. There are nine trains daily from 04.00 to around 18.30 and the journey takes between 30 and 50 minutes.

If travelling from Lille Flandres, take the TER Line 15 (Boulogne via Saint-Pol and Béthune). Trains are less frequent but the journey time is around the same.

TOURIST INFORMATION
Montreuil-sur-Mer Tourist Office 11–13 Rue Pierre Ledent; \ 03 21 06 04 27; w destinationmontreuilloisencotedopale.com;

 09.30–12.30 & 14.00–18.00 Mon–Sat, 10.00–13.00 & 15.00–17.00 Sun, may alter in winter

WHAT TO SEE AND DO
Museum of France Roger Rodière (\ 03 21 86 90 83; w musees-montreuilsurmer. fr; Feb–Mar & Oct–Nov 10.00–noon & 14.00–17.00 daily; Apr–Jun & Sep 10.00– noon & 14.00–18.00 daily; Aug 10.00–18.00 daily except Tue; adults/under 12s €5/free) This museum was opened in 1927 by a group of scholars, including the historian Roger Rodière, who believed in the importance of saving the history of Montreuil-sur-Mer and Montreuillois. Though it closed for more than 20 years, a second generation of historians in the late 1960s relaunched the development of a permanent exhibition space for the city's historical collections.

The museum now forms part of the fortified **La Citadelle,** which in 1916 became Field Marshal Douglas Haig's (see box, page 76) operational headquarters, supplying

La Citadelle, Montreuil-sur-Mer (IE/A)

FIELD MARSHAL SIR DOUGLAS HAIG

A former cavalry commander, Haig was born to a middle-class family in Edinburgh in 1861 and rose to become commander of the British Expeditionary Force (British Army) in 1915 until the end of the war. During the war his leadership wasn't faulted, but some historians now question his inability to alter tactics and embrace new technologies, which possibly led to the unnecessary deaths of millions of soldiers – many of the battles he led counted among the bloodiest of the entire war.

troops with provisions and equipment from Dunkerque, Calais and Boulogne for the Front in Flanders, Artois and the Somme.

Haig statue (*Pl du Théâtre*) In the centre of this square stands an equestrian statue of Field Marshal Douglas Haig (see box, above), who commandeered Beaurepaire House a few kilometres away and had a penchant for riding through the adjoining countryside. The statue was taken down during the German occupation in World War II, but locals recovered the original mould and recast a new one.

Haig statue, Montreuil-sur-Mer (Mc/WC)

9

The Somme

Of all the commemorations that took place, the one that best remembered those British who died in World War I was the centennial of the Battle of the Somme in July 2016. Attended by royals including the Duchess of Cornwall, whose great uncle Captain Harry Cubit died amid the 'foul brown mush, which swallows everything', the commemoration helped to give voice to a lost generation of many 'known unto God'. In the region, major World War I museums were opened, or expanded, while battlefield tours and Remembrance Trails by bike, on foot or even from the air, are now encouraging a younger generation to look behind the silence of the graves. The website w visit-somme.com/great-war provides a comprehensive guide to all World War I aspects in the Somme region.

BATTLEFIELD TOURS

14–18 Somme Battlefield Tours \03 22 76 52 21; w 14-18sommetours.com. Run by Bart Metselaar, who works exclusively with British & Dutch clients.
Battlefields Experience \03 22 76 29 60; w thebattleofthesomme.co.uk. Run by military historian Rod Bedford.
Bike France \04 75 81 06 08; w cyclingthewesternfront.co.uk
Chemins d'Histoire Battlefield Tours \03 23 67 77 64; w cheminsdhistoire.com. Bespoke or private tours themed according to your nationality.
Cobbers Battlefield Tours \06 87 43 10 49; w anzac-tours.jimdo.com. Small-group minibus

tours departing from the Somme 1916 Museum in Albert, including buggy & cycling tours. Led by Brit Colin Gillard.
Somme(r)–Ballade \03 22 75 25 01; w somme-r-ballade.jimdo.com. Somme walking tours led by Julia Maasen conducted in French, English & German.
Terres de Mémoire \03 22 84 23 05; w terresdememoire.com. Another 2-man team offering in-depth tours of the Somme.
True Blue Digger Tours \03 22 51 56 21; w trueblue-diggertours.com. Half- & full-day tours catering to Australians.

AMIENS

Surprisingly, World War I left the grand historic capital of Picardy relatively unscathed, despite it being a hive of war-related activity, from Germans seizing hostages here during the first months of the war to the Thanksgiving Mass held in its cathedral on 18 November 1918. There was even a guidebook about the great city on the Somme printed in English for soldiers.

GETTING THERE AND AWAY Coming **by car** from Calais, follow the E402/A16 south, past Boulogne-sur-Mer and Abbeville, to Amiens (*158km; approx 1hr 30mins*). From Calais, Lille or Paris-Gare du Nord, **trains** take approximately 1 hour to reach Amiens.

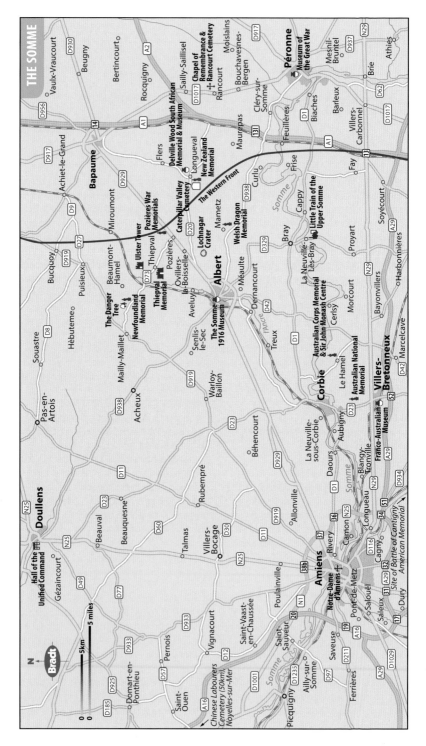

Vaux-Vraucourt

Beugny

D930

Bertincourt

Rocquigny

A2

Sailly-Saillisel

Moislains

Chapel of
Remembrance &
Rancourt Cemetery

Péronne

Museum of
the Great War

Mesnil-
Bruntel

D937

N29

Rancourt

Bouchavesnes-
Bergen

D1017

Brie

Athies

D956

Achiet-le-Grand

Bapaume

14

A1

Delville Wood South African
Memorial & Museum

Longueval

New Zealand
Memorial

Cléry-sur-
Somme

Barleux

D62

D1017

Feuillères

Blaches

D1

Villers-
Carbonnel

Flers

Maurepas

131

13

A1

D917

Miraumont

D929

Caterpillar Valley
Cemetery

The Western Front

Curlu

Fay

Soyécourt

A29

Bucquoy

Pozières War
Memorials

Mametz

Somme

Frise

Cappy

Proyart

Puisieux

D27

D919

Ulster Tower

Thiepval

Lochnagar
Crater

Welsh Dragon
Memorial

Bray

D329

Little Train of the
Upper Somme

La Neuville-
Lès-Bray

N29

Harbonnières

Beaumont-
Hamel

Pozières

Ovillers-
la-Boisselle

Albert

Méaulte

D938

Bayonvillers

Hébuterne

D73

The Danger
Tree

Thiepval
Memorial

Newfoundland
Memorial

Aveluy

Dernancourt

Cerisy

Morcourt

Marcelcave

Souastre

D8

Mailly-Maillet

Senlis-
le-Sec

The Somme
1916 Museum

D42

D1

Treux

Villers-
Bretonneux

D42

Pas-en-
Artois

Acheux

D938

Warloy-
Baillon

Corbie

Australian Corps Memorial
& Sir John Monash Centre

Le Hamel

Australian National
Memorial

D23

Franco-Australian
Museum

52

Béhencourt

D23

Aubigny

Daours

Blangy-
Tronville

D934

Beauval

D23

Rubempré

D929

La Neuville-
sous-Corbie

D1

Somme

N29

Longueau

34

51

Doullens

N25

Talmas

Villers-
Bocage

Allonville

D919

D11

Rivery

Camon

N25

D116

Cagny

32

Site of Battle of Cantigny
Dury American Memorial

Hall of the
Unified Command

N25

D49

Gézaincourt

D77

Beauquesne

D60

D30

D11

N25

37

36

Amiens

38

Notre-Dame
d'Amiens

Pont-de-Metz

31

A29

Saleux

Dury

17

Pernois

Poulainville

N1

20

Saint-Vaast-
en-Chaussée

Saint-
Sauveur

Salouël

19

A16

D933

D933

Vignacourt

D12

Saveuse

D211

A29

D1029

Domart-en-
Ponthieu

D57

Saint-
Ouen

D1001

Ailly-sur-
Somme

Ferrières

D925

D185

Chinese Labourers
Cemetery (50km)/
Noyelles-sur-Mer

A16

Picquigny

D1235

Somme

D97

TOURIST INFORMATION

Amiens Tourist Office 23 Pl Notre Dame; 03 22 71 60 50; w visit-amiens.com; Apr–Sep 09.30–18.30 Mon–Sat, 10.00–noon & 14.00–17.00 Sun; Oct–Mar 09.30–18.00 Mon–Sat, 10.00–noon & 14.00–17.00 Sun

The Somme Tourist Board 54 Rue St Fuscien; 03 22 71 22 71; e accueil@somme-tourisme.com; w visit-somme.com/great-war

WHAT TO SEE AND DO

Notre-Dame d'Amiens (*Pl Notre-Dame 30; 03 22 71 60 50; w cathedrale-amiens.fr; daily, tours Apr–Sep 14.00–17.00 Mon & Wed–Sun, Oct–Mar 14.00 & 15.00 Mon & Wed–Sun; adult/senior/under 18s €6/free/free*) This magnificent 13th-century church, the largest Gothic cathedral in France, miraculously escaped destruction during World War I. Pictures of the cathedral, and notably of the touching sculpture of *The Crying Angel*, regularly featured on postcards that soldiers sent home. Six Allied flags are displayed inside the edifice, while commemorative plaques pay tribute to Field Marshal Foch and General Leclerc and to the soldiers who fought in the Somme.

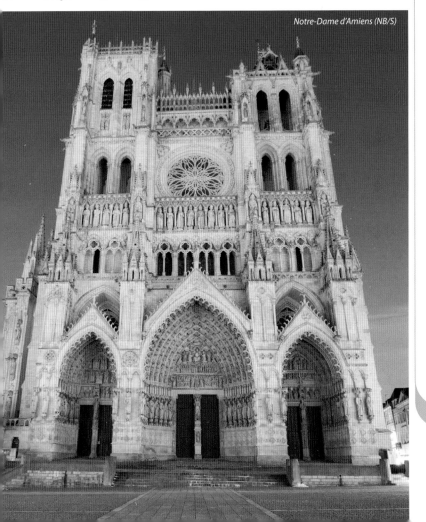

Notre-Dame d'Amiens (NB/S)

Up until 1916, the Somme just witnessed skirmishes. However, late in 1915, the Allies planned a set of major offensives against the Central Powers; the Franco-British were to focus on breaking through the Front Line in the Somme. At the same time, though, the German Army decided to switch its main attention from the Eastern to the Western Front, aiming to draw the French Army into a devastating battle around Verdun in early 1916 (see box, page 107). As a result, many French troops were sent east to the Meuse in the first half of the year, while the British Army became the principal Allied force involved in the Somme Offensive, which began on 1 July 1916.

It started when the vast **Lochnagar mine** (page 86) – one of 16 such mines laid by the British beneath German lines along the battle front – exploded 10 minutes ahead of the 07.30 start. Debris was flung almost a mile into the air, as graphically recorded by Royal Flying Corps pilot Cecil Lewis in his book *Sagittarius Rising*: 'The whole earth heaved and flared, a tremendous and magnificent column rose up into the sky.'

Moments after the explosion of these large mines, the British and French forces emerged from their trenches under cover of artillery fire. Despite inflicting considerable damage on some German strongpoints, progress proved elusive. By the end of the first day, 58,000 casualties were recorded, of whom 19,000 died. These casualties were the largest ever loss sustained by the British Army in a single day.

Spasmodic fighting continued until, with battlefields churned into a muddy morass, the respective armies settled into their winter quarters. After 4½ months, the British had advanced 12km. Of the three million soldiers from all sides recorded as having been sent to the Somme Front Line during this period, some 1.2 million were wounded, killed or went missing in action. To put this into perspective, at the time of writing, 444 British soldiers have been killed since 2001 in the Afghan War.

The Somme Offensive remains one of the most widely remembered battles of World War I, in part because, unlike the essentially Franco-German Battle of Verdun, it involved over 20 nationalities fighting or working on behalf of Great Britain, France and Germany. These included: Russian, Belgian, Chinese and Egyptian forces, individual Americans and, in 1918, American forces, as well as contingents from Montenegro, Romania, Switzerland, Sweden and Spanish Catalonia.

PÉRONNE

Péronne, a historic town on the Somme River with a medieval castle in the centre, was occupied by the Germans for much of World War I. As a result, the town was frequently bombarded. The French civilians here suffered terribly; almost 30% of residents became victims of the war. The Germans eventually left Péronne of their own accord in March 1917, but recaptured it in March 1918 during their Spring Offensive. It was finally liberated by Australian troops on 2 September 1918.

GETTING THERE AND AWAY Coming **by car** from Amiens, follow the E44/A29 east for 32km, then take exit 53 and merge on to the A1/E15/E19 north to Péronne (*66km; 50mins*). There is no **train station** in Péronne.

Péronne Tourist Office 1 Rue Louis XI; ☎ 03 22 84 42 38; w hautesomme-tourisme.com; ⊕ Jun–Sep 09.00–noon & 14.00–18.00 Mon–Sat; Jul–Aug 09.00–noon & 14.00–18.00 Mon–Sat, 09.00–12.30 Sun & public holidays; Oct–May 09.00–noon & 14.00–17.30 Mon–Sat, 09.00–noon & 14.00–17.00 Sun. Walking & hiking trails can be downloaded free at w visit-somme.com.

WHAT TO SEE AND DO

Museum of the Great War (Historial de la Grande Guerre) (*Château de Péronne;* ☎ *03 22 83 14 18;* w *historial.fr;* ⊕ *Apr–Sep 09.30–18.00 daily; Oct–Mar 09.30–17.00 Mon–Tue & Thu–Sun; adult/child 7–16/under 7s/student/family of 4 €10/5/free/4.50/25, combined ticket with Thiepval Museum adult/7–18/family of 4 €12/6/30; suitable for those with physical, mental or hearing disabilities;* ♿) Péronne's Historial de la Grande Guerre is one of the most important museums dedicated to World War I in France, and its website, conveniently linked with that at Thiepval (page 84), gives details of other battlefield sites. It occupies the remnants of the town's medieval castle, which have been greatly added to by the contemporary exhibition spaces created by architect Edouard Henri Ciriani. The coverage of World War I is in good part thematic, and the emphasis is put on the individuals involved in the terrible campaigns. The objects on display are in themselves often telling: for example, a German shovel laid alongside a French one, or a British private's trench clubs, testifying to the brutality of hand-to-hand fighting. Shared grief and competing memories emerge in many depictions, such as bronze carvings, statues and lithographs. The museum holds remarkable war etchings by German artist Otto Dix. Temporary exhibitions are regularly held here. The centre also has an **International Research Centre** for those tracing relatives. Contact Caroline Fontaine (☎ *03 22 83 54 13*).

Museum of the Great War, Péronne (T70/S)

The museum is now offering a virtual reality tour. Visitors scan the QR code on the display with their phone and point it towards the pits. The uniform in the pit then comes to life and a soldier appears, telling his story.

AROUND PÉRONNE

RANCOURT

The Chapel of Remembrance (*Route National 2;* ⏱ *09.30–12.30 & 14.00–18.00 Wed–Sun; free entry*) This substantial chapel, the one significant monument commemorating the French Army's participation in the Battle of the Somme, was built to remember the French soldiers who died in a violent communications-busting offensive around Rancourt, from September to November 1916. The impetus for the chapel's construction came from Marie Mathilde du Bos, née Johnston, originally from New Orleans. She was the mother of Jean du Bos, one of the fallen. There is now a permanent exhibition on religion during World War I inside. The largest French cemetery in the Somme spreads out around the chapel. There is a large German cemetery nearby, plus a small British one.

LONGUEVAL

Delville Wood South African National Memorial (*Lies off the D929 towards Calais & Lille, on the edge of Delville Wood*) Rows of oak trees grown from South African acorns lead to an arch recalling a terrible week in July 1916 when the 1st South African Brigade spent five nights and six days fighting the enemy in Delville Wood. Of the original 121 officers and 3,032 South African soldiers that fought here, only 142 emerged unscathed. In

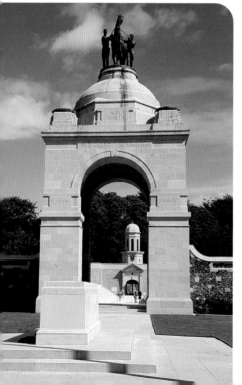

Delville Wood South African National Memorial (ST)

the grounds is the **South African Delville Wood Commemorative Museum** (*Route de Ginchy 5;* ☎ *03 22 85 02 17;* w *delvillewood. com;* ⏱ *Feb–mid Apr & mid-Oct–Nov 10.00–16.00 Tue–Sun, mid-Apr–mid-Oct 10.00–17.30 Tue–Sat, 10.00–17.00 Sun; free entry*). Set behind the national memorial, the National Museum highlights the role of all South Africans, black and white, on the various theatres of battle. This began on 30 June 2014 with the reburial of the first South African native labourer to have died during World War I, as black South African men at the time were forbidden to take up arms. Previously buried in a civilian cemetery in Bléville near Le Havre, his remains were reburied in the courtyard of the Delville Wood Cemetery across the road from the National Memorial. More than 21,000 black South Africans did, however, serve as labourers in France during the war. Behind the museum stands a scar-covered hornbeam, the sole survivor of the battle. On 12 July 2016, in commemoration of the centenary of the battle, a garden of remembrance was unveiled to remember 600 soldiers who have no known grave. A wall of remembrance was also uncovered to honour the South African servicemen of both the 1st South African Infantry Brigade and the South African Native Labour Contingent.

Artefacts and exhibitions concerning the sinking of the SS *Mendi* were added 100 years after the ship carrying hundreds of black South African men was sunk in the English Channel. The design of the museum was inspired by the Castle of Good Hope, the first European fortification erected in South Africa.

New Zealand Memorial and Caterpillar Valley Cemetery (*New Zealand Memorial just north of Longueval village, along a little road off the D197; Caterpillar Valley Cemetery not in Caterpillar Valley, but on the south side of the D20 between Longueval & Contalmaison; both ⊕ daily; free entry*) The Memorial obelisk pays homage to the New Zealand Division's role in the Somme Offensive from 15 September 1916, while the large Caterpillar Valley Cemetery also commemorates Kiwi soldiers who went missing through the Battle of the Somme. The names of 1,211 New Zealand and Maori soldiers with no known grave are engraved on a wall here.

ALBERT

Located on a major route through northern France, the town of Albert has been repeatedly destroyed down the centuries. In World War I it long lay close to the Front and the Germans bombarded it heavily throughout 1915. A German shell badly damaged the dome of the town's great 19th-century basilica, causing the gilded statue of the Virgin on the top to lean precariously, a position in which she was famously left for the rest of the war. The ruined town had to be wholly reconstructed after the conflict; the basilica was rebuilt in its original style.

GETTING THERE AND AWAY Coming **by car** from Amiens, follow the D929 east direct to Albert (*30km; 35mins*). From Amiens or Arras, **trains** take approximately 20 minutes.

TOURIST INFORMATION
Albert Tourist Office 9 Rue Léon Gambetta; `03 22 75 16 42; ⊕ w tourisme-paysducoquelicot. com; ⊕ 10.00–12.30 & 13.30–17.00 Mon–Fri, 10.00–12.30 & 14.00–17.00 Sat

WHAT TO SEE AND DO
The Somme 1916 Museum (Musée Somme 1916) (*Underground, reached from the right-hand side of the Basilica Notre-Dame de Brebières, Rue Anicet Godin; `03 22 75 16 17; w somme-trench-museum.co.uk; ⊕ 09.00–18.00 daily; adult/6–18/ under 6s €7.50/4.50/free*) Located inside a 13th-century tunnel that was repurposed as an air-raid shelter in 1938, this long gallery depicts the life of soldiers living in the trenches during the 1 July 1916 Offensive and concludes with a sound display of a bombardment.

AROUND ALBERT

THIEPVAL Thiepval's role in the Battle of the Somme was strategic, with the Germans building a major line of defence around the village. Captured by British troops on 27 September 1916, retaken by the Germans in March 1918, it was finally recaptured by the British in August the same year.

Thiepval Memorial (JNP/S)

Thiepval Memorial and Visitor Centre (*Follow Rue de L'Ancre from Thiepval village*) The largest British war memorial in the world, the massive Thiepval Memorial to the Missing reaches 45m in height. Designed by Sir Edwin Lutyens and built between 1929 and 1932, it caused controversy when it was constructed because of the cost. Most movingly, its many towering sides are covered with the names of over 72,000 British and South African soldiers with no known graves – the so-called 'Missing of the Somme' – who died in battles between July 1915 and March 1918. However, 90% of those recalled died between July and November 1916. Annual commemorative ceremonies are held here on 1 July and 11 November.

The visitor centre (admission free) features an educational exhibition about the war and in particular the Battle of the Somme and Thiepval itself. A screening room shows three films: *Somme in the Great War*, *Memory* and *Thiepval*. A computer database is available to research soldiers who died in the war or locate a cemetery or memorial.

Thiepval Museum (*8 Rue de l'Ancre;* ☎ *03 22 74 60 47;* w *historial.org;* ⊕ *Mar–Oct 09.30–18.00 daily, Nov–Feb 09.30–17.00 daily; adult/child €6/3; combined ticket for the Museums of Péronne & Thiepval adult/7–16/under 7s/family of 4 €12/6/free/30*) Inaugurated with a flourish on 2 June 2016, to mark the centenary of the Battle of the Somme, this high-tech expansion of the nearby visitor centre (see above) lies at the very heart of the battlefields.

Managed – as with Péronne – by Historial, Museum of the Great War, the museum's permanent exhibition displays artefacts, archaeological finds, multimedia displays and life-size installations, and a replica of *Old Charles*, the plane flown by Georges Guynemer, a top French fighter ace with 54 victories to his name.

There's also a 60m-long panoramic mural, which is printed on to back-lit glass, by Joe Sacco, a famous Maltese-American cartoonist and illustrator. The mural provides an hour-by-hour account of the Battle of the Somme (see box, page 80) on 1 July. In the centre, a pit displays archaeological finds and World War I artefacts.

At the entrance, a large animated map with period photographs and film presents the impact of the fighting on the Somme.

Ulster Tower (Tour d'Ulster) and Visitor Centre (*Route de St Pierre Divion, Thiepval;* ☎ *03 22 74 87 14;* w *sommeassociation.com/visit/ulster-memorial-tower;* ⊕ *site: 10.00–17.00 Tue–Sun, tower: Mar–Nov 10.00–17.00 Tue–Sun; free*) A replica of Helen's Tower from the Clandeboye Estate in County Down, Ireland, the 21m-tall Ulster Tower marks the spot from where troops of the 36th Ulster Division advanced on the German Front Line on the initial 1 July 1916 Somme Offensive. They suffered over 5,000 casualties, with approximately one man in four killed, injured, missing or taken prisoner. Nine Victoria Crosses were awarded.

The small museum beside the tower gives some further information on the fighting in these parts and has some rare personal items on display. Original trenches inside Thiepval Wood, which mark the Front-Line battleground of the 36th (Ulster) Division, have been excavated during ongoing preservation work.

BEAUMONT-HAMEL This village north of Thiepval, set above the Ancre Valley, had been heavily fortified by the Germans prior to the start of the Somme Offensive.

Newfoundland Memorial and Beaumont-Hamel Visitor Centre (*On route D73 approximately 1.5km southeast of Auchonvillers;* ⏲ *Apr–Sep noon–18.00 Mon, 10.00–18.00 Tue–Sun; Oct–Mar 11.00–17.00 Mon, 09.00–17.00 Tue–Sun; free entry*) Beaumont-Hamel lay on the northern end of the section of the Front that was chosen for the Somme Offensive, which began on 1 July 1916 (see box, page 80). A massive mine planted by British engineers went off nearby at 07.20 that morning, 10 minutes before the assault, rather than 2 minutes before, like the other mines laid along the line. This early warning, along with the Germans' high position, allowed them to mow down the soldiers of the Newfoundland Regiment as they emerged from their trenches close by. After 30 minutes, only 110 out of 780 men remained unharmed in one of the most devastating actions on the first day of the Battle of the Somme.

After the war, the Dominion of Newfoundland bought the land where the regiment had been stationed and preserved it. Visitors can therefore walk through one of the clearest extant network of trenches. Various memorials not just to the Newfoundland Regiment stand scattered about the park, but none is more striking than the bronze statue of a caribou, the Newfoundland Division's emblem, standing atop a mound looking out towards the German lines. At the base, three bronze plaques commemorate 820 men from the regiment, the Newfoundland Royal Naval Reserves and the Mercantile Marine who died in World War I and whose bodies have never been found. Look out for the skeleton of the Danger Tree, the only one that survived the devastation in the area.

The **visitor centre** (☏ *03 22 76 70 86;* w *veterans.gc.ca;* ⏲ *09.00–17.00 daily (11.00 Mon); free entry*) traces the history of the Newfoundland Regiment and some of its characters, alongside displays of memorabilia and video snippets.

POZIÈRES As the Somme Offensive evolved through July 1916, Australian troops were heavily involved in the task of securing Pozières and its high, well-defended ridge, which was a key obstacle to capturing the vital Thiepval Ridge. In the fierce fighting that month, the three Australian Divisions involved lost over a third of their men.

Newfoundland Memorial, Beaumont-Hamel (AB/ST)

Pozières War Memorials (*Along the D929 Albert–Bapaume road*) There are two important Australian memorials at Pozières: one to the 2nd Division at the highest point on Pozières Ridge, where a windmill once stood, and one to the 1st Division at Gibraltar. On the opposite side of the busy road, the **Tank Corps Memorial** recalls the first-ever use of a tank in battle, at Flers-Courcelette, on 15 September 1916. As to the separate, impressively colonnaded **Pozières Memorial**, it lists the names of 14,692 British and South African soldiers with no known graves who died in the Second Battle of the Somme between 21 March and 8 August 1918. Every year, Digger Cote 160, an association of local people from Pozières (w *digger-pozieres.org*), stages war performances in the village.

Walking trails Two new walking trails link sites of particular significance in and around the village, and a self-guided tour is provided with the Australians at Pozières app. Stop off for a cuppa at Le Tommy Restaurant & Museum 1916 located on the main road off Pozières, where many Australian Digger photos can be seen on the walls.

OVILLERS-LA-BOISELLE
Lochnagar Crater (w *lochnagarcrater.org*) Caused by British mines set off at the very outset of the Somme Offensive, Lochnagar Crater is on a staggering scale, being 100.5m wide and 21m deep, making it one of the largest wartime craters ever created. It is looked after by a passionate British man, Richard Dunning, who bought the site in 1978 and allows visitors to see it for free, although he is grateful for donations. A duckboard trail allows you to walk around the rim. Look out for a plaque on the walkway dedicated to Sister Ellen Andrews – a reminder of the nurses who failed to return.

MAMETZ
Although the village of Mametz was captured by the British 7th Division on 1 July 1916, further progress was blocked by heavy German resistance in Mametz Wood, which was taken on 12 July after heavy losses by the 38th Welsh Division. The poet Siegfried Sassoon, then an officer in the 2nd Battalion Royal Welsh Fusiliers, described Mametz Wood as: 'looming on the opposite slope…a dense wood of old trees and undergrowth…a menacing wall of gloom.' He was awarded the Military Cross for bravery.

The Welsh Dragon Memorial of the 38th Division (*From Mametz village, take the road towards Contalmaison & follow signs in Welsh to the memorial;* w *tourisme-paysducoquelicot.com; free entry*) Inaugurated on 11 July 1987, the monument to

Lochnagar Crater (KG/S)

The Welsh Dragon Memorial of the 38th Division (CA/ST)

the 38th Welsh Division is the Red Dragon of Wales, its wings held aloft and its claws clutching pieces of barbed wire.

LA NEUVILLE-LÈS-BRAY

Little Train of the Upper Somme (*Hameau de Froissy, 80340 La Neuville-lès-Bray;* \ *03 22 76 14 60;* w *petittrainhautesomme.fr;* ☉ *museum: May–Jun 13.30–18.00 Sun, 8 Jul–27 Aug 14.00–17.45 Tue–Thu & Sat–Sun; for train departure times consult website; adult/5–12/under 5s €10.50/7/free*) Railway buffs enjoy this narrow-gauge line built in 1916 for the Battle of the Somme and used to supply the trenches with weapons. On part of the one-hour, 14km journey between Froissy and Dompierre, you follow the Somme River itself.

The railway's **museum** at Froissy (*when trains are running*) displays many locomotives and wagons, including French, German and American ones, mostly from the 1910s and the 1920s. There's a car park, gift shop and toilets. The train is situated in the hamlet of Froissy (a little village, not indicated on maps), 3km south of Bray-sur-Somme on the D329 road. If you use a satnav, make sure to choose the right Froissy – there's another one in Oise department, an hour away.

LE HAMEL

Australian Corps Memorial (*Chemin de Sailly Laurette, east out of Le Hamel village centre*) This memorial marks the successful battle on 4 July 1918, when General Sir John Monash (page 88), one of the most creative and forward-thinking generals in World War I, led his Australian and American troops into a clash that lasted only 93 minutes. Take a look at the German trench as well as the 20 information panels around the site.

VILLERS–BRETONNEUX
It was here that Aussie soldiers stopped the German push in April 1918, preventing Amiens from being captured.

Australian National Memorial (*beside the D23 road c2km north of Villers-Bretonneux towards Corbie;*

LE HAMEL ON HORSEBACK

Explore Le Hamel and the Australian battlefields by horse and carriage on 1½-hour **tours** (\ *03 22 96 03 16;* w *penseedelehamel. blog4ever.com; €25pp*).

free entry) Designed by famous architect Sir Edwin Lutyens – who also designed the Thiepval Memorial (page 84) – and inaugurated by King George VI in July 1938, this memorial marks the names of missing Australian soldiers from World War I. Many of the 10,982 names originally displayed have since been identified and the work is ongoing. At the time of writing, there are now 10,729 Australian servicemen officially commemorated.

Sir John Monash Centre (*Route de Villiers-Bretonneux, 808000 Fouilloy;* \ *03 60 62 01 40;* w *sjmc.gov.au;* ⊕ *10.00–17.00 daily; free entry*) Melbourne-born Sir John Monash was an outstanding military and civilian leader credited with shortening World War I thanks to his major victories while in command of the Australian Army Corps in France.

Located within the grounds of the Australian National Memorial and military cemetery and commissioned and financed by the Australian government's Department of Veterans' Affairs, the Sir John Monash Centre commemorates the 295,000 men and women who served on the Western Front, of whom 46,000 never returned.

The interior is a hive of multimedia galleries, including the immersive 186-screen, 360-degree 'Watchout' experience that uses smoke effects and light beams to throw visitors into the bewildering chaos of combat as Australian soldiers engage in the battles of Villers-Bretonneux and Le Hamel.

For children, the centre provides tablets loaded with the Digger Quest app (suitable for 6 years-plus) that uses Australian totems, such as a kangaroo or an emu, to help explain Australia's involvement in World War I via educational games. Adults can download the SJMC app to their own smartphones (bring your own earphones).

Sir John Monash Centre (F/A/A)

Franco-Australian Museum (Musée Franco-Australien) (*9 Rue Victoria;* ☎ *03 22 96 80 79;* w *museeaustralien.com;* ⊕ *Apr–Oct 09.30–17.30 daily, Nov–Mar 09.30–16.30 daily, closed last week Dec & 1st week Jan; adult/11–18/under 11s €6/3/free*) Created by the Franco-Australian Association in 1975 – and entirely renovated in 2016 – the museum is located on the first floor of the town's Victoria School, itself rebuilt in the 1920s using donations from schoolchildren in Victoria, Australia. A large part of its collection was acquired through donations made to the Franco-Australian Association. Soldiers' personal effects (uniforms, letters and photographs) and moving accounts themed on Franco-Australian friendship help visitors to understand the relationship forged between the two countries. Midway through the museum, a glass-roofed, chapel-like area enables visitors to see and contemplate the message of thanks. The Victoria Hall displays Australian wildlife and an exhibition of photos from the state: carvings are the work of Australian artist John Grant and his students. In the schoolyard a large sign reads 'Do Not Forget Australia'. An Australian fresco was created by the staff and children of the school and inaugurated on Anzac Day in 2009.

DOULLENS

HALL OF THE UNIFIED COMMAND (*1st flr of Hôtel de Ville, 2 Av du Maréchal Foch;* ☎ *03 22 32 54 52;* w *tourisme-territoirenordpicardie.com/home/hall-of-sole-command;* ⊕ *10.00–12.30 & 14.00–16.00 Mon–Fri, 10.00–noon Sat; free entry*) It was here on 26 March 1918 that, at the behest of General Haig (see box, page 76), the French and British governments appointed General Foch to take over as Commander in Chief of military strategy. On 8 August, he launched his final counteroffensive, which led to the Armistice being signed on 11 November 1918.

CANTIGNY

AMERICAN MEMORIAL (*In the centre of the village*) This memorial marks the thousand-plus casualties of the 1st American Division and 28th American Infantry Regiment at the Battle of Cantigny between 28 and 31 May 1918. This was the first major American offensive of the war and not only did it contain the German's Spring Offensive, it also raised Allied morale and showed the competence of the US soldiers, which was further displayed by the American Army and Marine Corps in subsequent campaigns during 1918.

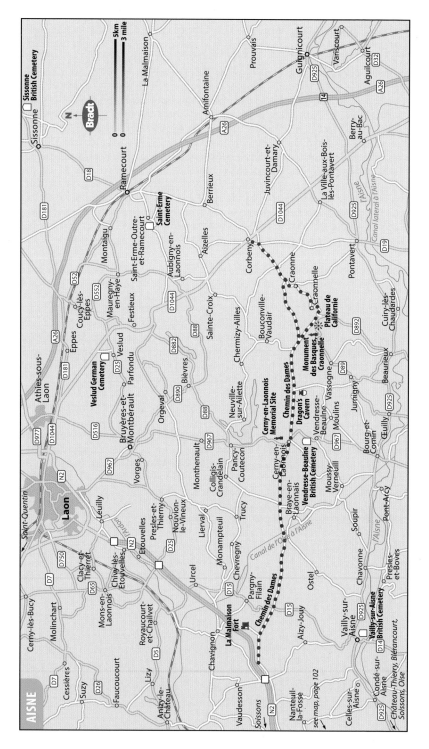

10

Aisne

Overshadowed by the slaughter at the Battle of the Somme (see box, page 80), in fact, Aisne, the Picardy *département* (or county) east of the Somme, also suffered terrible destruction through World War I, when its wooded landscapes became a permanent battleground. Most atrocious was the protracted conflict between German and French forces for control of the Chemin des Dames Ridge. It was in Aisne that the first trenches were dug in 1914.

LAON

As *département* or county capital of Aisne, the medieval town of Laon is a good base from which to explore nearby wartime sites. The city remained in German hands throughout the war.

GETTING THERE AND AWAY From Calais **by car**, follow the E15/A26 southeast to Arras, then the E17/A26 continues past Saint-Quentin to Laon (*225km; approx 3hrs*). If travelling from Belgium, follow the E19/A2 west down to Cambrai, then pick up the E17/A26 to Laon (*approx 1hr 40mins*). **Trains** depart regularly from Paris Gare du Nord (*1hr 30mins*), Reims (*35mins*) and Saint-Quentin (*50mins*).

TOURIST INFORMATION

Laon Tourist Office Hôtel Dieu, Pl du Parvis Gautier de Mortagne; ☏ 03 23 20 28 62; w tourisme-paysdelaon.com; ◷ Jul–Aug

10.00–18.00 daily, Sep–Jun 10.00–12.30 & 13.30–18.00 daily

AROUND LAON

Veslud German Cemetery (*Take the A26/E15 signposted Reims–Paris & continue to Saint-Quentin, then junction 13 for the N2 & D1044; the cemetery sits beside Veslud Church; w memorial-chemindesdames.fr*) This communal cemetery contains the graves of 1,704 German soldiers who were buried here after the April 1917 Chemin des Dames Offensive. In 1979, the old wooden crosses were replaced with stone crosses or stelae (inscribed stone slabs).

Saint-Erme Cemetery (*Rue du Monument, Saint-Erme; follow the D1044 south for 11km, then turn left on to the D90 signposted for Saint-Erme. Once there turn left at the T-junction in the direction of Ramecourt & take the 2nd exit marked 'Toutes Directions' & look out for the cemetery sign; ◷ 09.00–17.00 daily; free entry*) Encircled by a rubble wall, this cemetery is hidden down a 30m pathway off the main road. Look for the Commonwealth War Graves Commission sign at the entrance. An extension of the local communal cemetery, it contains the bodies of

Sissonne British Cemetery (H/WC)

76 Commonwealth soldiers, seven of which remain unidentified. Of these, 36 were moved here from the Ramecourt Communal Cemetery.

Sissonne British Cemetery (*La Garenne des Cheneaux, Sissonne; follow the D1044 for 2.8km, then branch left on to the D181 crossing over the E17/A26 motorway, through Sissonne village; the memorial is 1km on the right – look for the tall white cross;* ⏱ *09.00–17.00 daily; free entry*) This small, pretty cemetery was built after the 1918 Armistice to bring together smaller cemeteries created after the bitter fighting at the Chemin des Dames. Today, there are 291 Commonwealth graves here, of which 127 are unidentified. Sissonne was occupied by the Germans throughout the war and next door is a German cemetery which, like the British, is made up of numerous congregated burial sites.

CHEMIN DES DAMES

The Chemin des Dames (w *chemindesdames.fr; take the N2 & follow the D18 for the main sites*) – now the D18CD road – is a 30km-long route along a narrow and

View of the Chemin des Dames (FXD/AT)

fertile plateau some 50km south of Laon, which rises between the valleys of the Aisne and Ailette rivers. It's here that soldiers of the British Expeditionary Force dug their first trenches on 14 September 1914. For some, it would come to be as relevant to World War I history as Flanders or the Somme.

Now tranquil, this area is littered with military cemeteries and monuments in honour of the 100,000 soldiers who died fighting over the 100m-high ridge. Famed for its stunning views (you can see Laon Cathedral from the top), the Chemin des Dames has seen military action in many periods of history: in 57BC, 100,000 Gauls fought Caesar's legions here; on 7 March 1814, Napoleon fought a battle here; and in September 1914, the Germans – retreating from the fiercely fought Battle of the Marne (page 104) – used the ridge to create an elaborate system of bunkers and machine-gun nests.

Despite this, and the impregnable nature of the terrain, the French General Robert Nivelle launched the futile Nivelle Offensive in freezing weather on 16 April 1917, in a bid to end the trench warfare. It was originally planned to commit nearly one million men in the battle, including 10,000 Senegalese infantry and 20,000 Russians. It ended in a bloody defeat, with mutinies breaking out in the French Army because of the general's stubborn refusal to call off the offensive. The casualties included 187,000 French and 163,000 Germans wounded, killed or missing. In May, General Nivelle was replaced by Marshal Philippe Pétain, whose troops captured La Malmaison Fort (page 95) on the road to Paris on 23 October 1917, leaving the defeated Germans retreating from the plateau to the north of the Ailette River.

TOURIST INFORMATION The closest tourist offices are located in **Laon** (page 91) and **Soissons** (page 96). Information is also available on w chemindesdames.fr.

WHAT TO SEE AND DO
Dragon's Cavern (Caverne du Dragon) and Chemin des Dames Museum (*Oulches–La-Vallée-Foulon, off the D18;* ☎ *03 23 25 14 18;* w *chemindesdames.fr;* ⊙ *1 Apr–14 Nov 10.00–18.00 daily; adult/under 18s €10/6; guided tours last 1hr 30mins & depart every 30/40mins in season, tour in English every day at noon*) In 1914, this site was known as the Ferme de la Creute because it backed on to one of the area's many old quarries (*creutes*). It was the only position the French would hold on the Chemin des Dames, but on 25 January 1915 it was snatched back by the Germans.

War debris at Dragon's Cavern (AH/A)

The French were finally able to recapture it on 25 June 1917 using gas, but the following month it was in good part back in German hands, who used it to strengthen their defences. This involved digging new galleries to reach the north of the ridge and installing barracks and a first-aid station with electric lighting.

For several months the opposing forces lived alongside each other in the darkness, spying on each other through a wall built in the galleries. Today, visitors can visit those very same galleries and experience first-hand the (albeit boarded) passageways where, wrote a French soldier, 'one crawls amid unimaginable debris… in a darkness that our lamps could hardly pierce, surrounded by the sickening stench of gas and dead bodies.' This is a long way from today's multimedia museum whose high-tech approach, with a variety of gizmos, is aimed at attracting (as with others in this guide) a family audience, while still educating new generations to the traumas of war. Guided tours of the underground quarry vie for interest with a 'Museum Survey' in which youngsters and parents have an hour to discover hidden objects. Others introduce visitors to the surrounding territory. Concerts, poetry and exhibitions of war-related topics bring a thoughtful contemporary touch to the living memorial.

Monument des Basques (*Between Craonnelle and Oulches-La Vallée Foulon;* w *chemindesdames.fr*) Located on a small slip road just off the Chemin des Dames road, this memorial pillar was built in 1928 as a tribute to soldiers of the French 36th Infantry Division who suffered significant losses in the Chemin des Dames fighting in the Plateau de Californie and Craonne area. The architect Mathieu Forest and sculptor Claude Grange were themselves veterans of the war.

ANTI-WAR SONG BANNED UNTIL 1974

The *Chanson de Craonne* was an anti-war song that was banned from being sung until as late as 1974. Originally called the *Chanson de Lorette*, it was published under this name in 1919 by journalist Paul Vaillant-Couturier in his book *La Guerre des soldats*. You can see why it didn't go down well: the first verse reads:

Goodbye life, goodbye love
Goodbye to all women,
It's over now, It's over forever
Since this loathsome war.

We have to leave our skins,
On the Craonne ridge,
'Cause we are all doomed to die,
We're the sacrificial victims.

Craonne (*From Laon, follow the D1044 south for 18km, then at Corbeny turn right on to the D18CD*) The historic village of Craonne was completely obliterated by artillery fire during World War I. Interestingly, the 'Song of Craonne' – written by an anonymous French soldier in 1917 – is still one of pacifism's great hymns. A wooded area marks the start of a 20-minute walk which takes you past the Tree of Peace site, erected by a local school, and offers views over the Plateau de Californie. Pick up a map from the tourist office or download a self-guided PDF map of the Vieux Craonne walk from w randonner.fr.

Plateau de Californie This 2.5km walk along the Chemin des Dames Ridge is lined with World War I information panels and offers terrific views of the Aisne Valley. Once the site of a farm – dubbed La Californie after its owner left for America to sell champagne – the plateau was the scene of fierce fighting when the Germans launched a surprise attack on British units on 27 May 1918. Underground galleries linked it to major positions, including the Dragon's Cavern (page 93). After the war, not a single tree was left standing. A 25m-high observatory allows you to contemplate the battlefield and see all the way to Reims. You can download a self-guided PDF map of the Belvédère du Plateau de Californie walk from w randonner.fr.

Cerny-en-Laonnois Memorial Site (*Grande Rue, just off the Chemin des Dames in the village of Cerny-en-Laonnois;* w *chemindesdames.fr*) Cerny was close to the Front Line and one of the most contested points of the war, remaining under German control until May 1917. It was destroyed by the battles for Chemin des Dames and had to be completely rebuilt after the war. Today, this sprawling site contains a French cemetery home to 5,150 combatants under flowered squares, including Senegalese and Malagasy fighters who fell during the Nivelles Offensive as well as an ossuary housing the remains of 2,386 soldiers. Behind the French cemetery is a German cemetery with 7,526 graves, including nearly 4,000 in the ossuary, and, at the back, a memorial chapel dedicated to reconciliation and a British monument.

Cerny–Laonnois Memorial (AD2/AT)

Vendresse-Beaulne British Cemetery (*Follow the D967 16km south of Laon, the cemetery is 800m north of the village on the west side of the road going towards Laon; ⊕ daily; free entry*) Located on the ridge flank, this cemetery contains 700 British graves of which only 327 are identified; some simply bear the words 'buried near this spot'. The neighbourhood of Vendresse-et-Troyon saw severe fighting in which British troops took part.

La Malmaison Fort (*Route départementale 18, Chavignon, follow the D18CD*) Ironically, the fort – one of a string of frontier fortifications built after France's 1870 defeat in the Franco-Prussian war – had

Monument des Anglais, Soissons (SCa/A)

been decommissioned in 1912. It was as central to the fighting as Fort de Condé (see below).

Driving and walking excursions The tourist office has self-guided PDF maps for a 25-minute circular drive taking in the main sights and 12km walks for walkers and mountain bikers, as well as a shorter 20-minute walk.

SOISSONS

Built beside the Aisne River, Soissons is one of the most ancient towns in northern France. It was here, in August 1914, that the British Expeditionary Force crossed the Aisne, and for the next 3½ years, French forces held this part of the Front until it was lost to the Germans in spring 1918. It was recaptured following the Battle of Soissons, 18–22 July 1918, involving French and British Divisions and the 1st and 2nd Infantry Divisions (United States), which were under French command.

GETTING THERE AND AWAY From Laon **by car**, follow the N2/D23 southwest for 29km then turn right on to the N31 to Soissons centre (*approx 35mins*). There are **trains** from Paris Gare du Nord (*1hr 15mins*) and direct trains from Laon (*26min*).

TOURIST INFORMATION
Soissons Tourist Office Pl Fernand Marquigny; 03 23 53 17 37; w tourisme-soissons.com; May–Sep 10.00–18.00 Mon–Sat, 10.00–12.15 & 13.15–17.00 Sun; Oct–Apr 10.00–17.00 Mon–Fri, 10.00–13.00 & 14.00–17.00 Sat

WHAT TO SEE AND DO
Monument des Anglais (*Crossroads of Rue Charpentier & Rue du Pot d'Étan; Soissons town centre*) Built in massive white Portland stone and featuring three stout soldiers, this memorial commemorates the 4,000 British officers and men who died in the Battles of the Aisne and Marne in 1918 but who have no known grave. You can see it from outside the low wrought-iron gates, but to gain full access you need to get a digital security code obtainable from the Commonwealth War Graves France Area Office (03 21 21 77 00; 10.00–16.00 Mon–Fri.)

AROUND SOISSONS
Fort de Condé (*Chivres-Val;* 03 23 54 40 00; w fortdeconde.com; 15 Apr–15 Nov 09.30–17.30 Tue–Sun, Jun–Aug 09.30–18.30 Tue–Sun; adults/8–17/under 8s/family

ticket (2 adults, 2 children) €6.50/4/free/€17; guided 1hr tours at 14.00 & 16.00 on Wed, Sat & Sun except on event days) Held by the Germans from September 1914 to April 1917, it was here that the French eventually welcomed General Pershing's US troops in their push on La Malmaison Fort. Condé was reoccupied by the Germans at the end of May 1918. They broke through Allied positions in just a few hours, dislodging the French and British soldiers in a deluge of fire. It was to be Germany's last major victory of World War I. By 8 August, the fort was reclaimed by the French 54th Infantry Regiment.

This museum is another case of wanting to attract all ages. In a game of Mission Impossible, youngsters have 45 minutes to find a code, which will save the fort on their first assignment as a young captain in 1886. More seriously, a 3D room, opened in 2017, shows the fragile traces of inscriptions, engravings and sculptures left by soldiers depicting the women they loved, their attachment to their pet and, above all, their humour. These are fast disappearing and with the quarries too dangerous to enter, this is yet another example of how wartime heritage is increasingly being preserved through images.

Vailly-sur-Aisne British Cemetery (*13km east of Soissons; the cemetery is on the left side shortly after entering Vailly-sur-Aisne town;* ⊕ *daily; free entry)* Lying on the north bank of the Aisne River, this cemetery contains the graves of 675 British soldiers, as well as bodies from other cemeteries. Of these, 328 gravestones still remain, with 40 headstones showing that the bodies were never found. Though most died fighting along the Chemin des Dames in September 1914, it is also the final resting place for over 60 Commonwealth soldiers who perished in summer 1918.

Carrières de Confrécourt (*Meeting point at Croix-Brisée, just west of Nouvron-Vingre village; visit by appointment only, email* e *soissonnais1418@laposte.net;* w *soissonnais14-8.fr/sites/visiter-les-sites;* ⊕ *2hr guided tours Mar–Sep 1st Sun of the month; adult/under 18s €5/free; wear sturdy shoes)* These quarries, now linked with local war-related talks and exhibitions, situated 10km from Soissons, are preserved by the World War I Association Soissonnais. They provided shelter for French soldiers from September 1914 onwards. The quarry walls are engraved with an assortment of graffiti and numerous personal belongings have been found here too. While ploughing his fields, local farmer Jean-Luc Pamart uncovered the bodies of numerous French soldiers who disappeared while defending the line on the banks of the Aisne, and the discovery was part of a BBC documentary. 'The soldiers would be down here for three days at a time,' Jean-Luc told the programme makers. 'So close to the misery and desolation of the battlefields above, and yet they sculpted such magnificent things – and with such limited resources. They were not grandiose works of art,' he added,

Fort de Condé (PG/A)

'but of the heart, of pure emotion, produced in the most tragic circumstances. Some of them were drawn in pencil but were never finished.' A chapel sits on site too.

Musée Franco-Américain du Château de Blérancourt (*Pl du Général Leclerc;* ☏ *03 23 39 60 16;* w *museefrancoamericain.fr/en;* ⊕ *Castle: 10.00–noon & 14.00–18.00 Mon & Wed–Sun (last admission 11.45 & 17.15), adult/concession/ under 26 €6/4.50/free, audio guide €1;* ⊕ *Gardens: 08.00–19.00 daily, free; ask about discounted combined tickets with Chateau de Coucy*) Located inside a 17th-century castle, this museum celebrates French–American friendship and features a section on American philanthropist Anne Morgan (daughter of famous banker JP Morgan), who established the humanitarian American Committee for Devastated France here in July 1917, bringing aid to the surrounding villages. Fighting forced them out in March 1918 and damaged the castle badly. The organisation bought the castle in 1919 and restored it. The extensive gardens are lovely too.

Somme American Cemetery and Memorial, Quennemont (AI/S)

Château de Coucy (*Rue du Château, Coucy-le-Château-Auffrique;* ☏ *03 23 52 71 28;* w *chateau-coucy.fr/en;* ⊕ *2 May–4 Sep 10.00–13.00 & 14.00–18.00 daily; 5 Sep–30 Apr 10.00–13.00 & 14.00–17.30 daily; adults/under 18s €6/ free; ask about combined tickets with Musée Franco–Américan du Château de Blérancourt*) Various German dignitaries, possibly even the Kaiser himself, were said to have frequented this vast medieval stronghold that was renovated in the 19th century and became a German military outpost on 1 September 1914. In March 1917, the keep and four towers were destroyed, whether for military purposes or merely as an act of vandalism is not known. However, it caused such a public uproar that a month later the ruins were declared 'a memorial to barbarity'. War reparations were used to clear the towers and to consolidate the wall. From the top of the castle you can see for 40km in every direction. Visitors can take a guided tour of the little town of Coucy-le-Château and learn about its occupation during World War I; ask at the tourist office (page 96). To get there from Laon, follow the D5 west for 20km (*approx 45mins*).

SAINT-QUENTIN

From 28 October 1914 to 1 October 1918, Saint-Quentin was a logistical hub for the German Army – even the street names were 'Germanised'. During occupation, all means of communicating with the rest of the country were prohibited and the townsfolk were forced to provide food for German troops. Food shortages resulted in deficiencies and disease among the French residents and there were fines for those who refused to comply. Some girls were rounded up to work in brothels, while children were forced to work in the fields or factory workshops.

On 1 October 1918, poet-soldier Wilfred Owen complained in his writings that Saint-Quentin was virtually inaccessible behind its rows of barbed wire – just before the city fell into the hands of French and British troops. They were astounded by what they saw, with 80% of the town destroyed, and only 253 people remaining.

GETTING THERE AND AWAY Saint-Quentin stands alongside the E17/A26 between Arras and Laon. It is also connected directly to Amiens via the E44/A29. Two fast **trains** depart from Laon each day with a change at Tergnier (*50mins*).

TOURIST INFORMATION

Saint-Quentin Tourist Office 3 Rue Émile Zola; 03 23 67 05 00; w destination-saintquentin.fr/en; 13.30–18.00 Mon, 09.00–noon & 13.30–18.00 Tue–Fri, 09.30–12.30 & 14.00–18.00 Sat, 13.30–17.30 Sun. For a guided tour, consult Paths of History (see below) who are based in town.

GUIDED TOURS

Paths of History e contact@cheminsdhistoire. com; w cheminsdhistoire.com, theobservationpost.com. Tailor-made tours based on the life of a soldier, unit, nationality or a specific site, led by World War I expert Olivier Dirson.

WHAT TO SEE AND DO

Monument Pont de Riqueval (*9.5km north of Saint-Quentin off the D1044*) On 29 September 1918, Captain Charlton of the British 1/6th North Staffordshire Regiment and soldiers in the Royal Engineers blocked this bridge, foiling German attempts to blow it up, granting the Allies control over the canal area around the village of Bellenglise. A photo taken of the fighting by an official British war photographer, David McLellan, can be seen at London's Imperial War Museum.

AROUND SAINT-QUENTIN

Somme American Cemetery and Memorial (*Quennemont; 1.5km southwest of Bony;* 09.00–17.00 daily; free entry) This cemetery pays tribute to the vital role Americans played in Aisne. Stark white crosses mark the graves of 1,884 US servicemen who were killed while serving in units attached to the British Army. The outer walls of the chapel, whose large bronze doors sport an American eagle, feature sculptured pieces of military equipment.

CHÂTEAU-THIERRY

Château-Thierry stands at a strategic point on the Aisne River between Paris and Reims. It experienced heavy fighting in 1918, particularly between American and German troops.

GETTING THERE AND AWAY If coming **by car,** Château-Thierry lies off the E50/A4 motorway linking Paris and Reims (*1hr 10mins*). Direct **trains** from Paris Gare de L'Est take 50 minutes; trains from Reims take about an hour.

TOURIST INFORMATION

Château-Thierry Tourist Office Rue Vallée 9; 03 23 83 51 14; w lesportesdelachampagne. com; 10.00–12.30 & 13.30–17.00 Mon–Wed & Fri–Sat, 11.00–12.30 & 13.30–17.00 Thu, 13.30–17.00 Sun & public holidays

WHAT TO SEE AND DO

American Monument/Château-Thierry Monument, Hill 204 (*Rue de la Côte 204; w abmc.gov/Chateau-Thierry* 07.00–20.00 daily; free entry) This imposing

10

granite monument overlooks the Marne River valley and is a mark of American–French friendship. The Hill 204 monument commemorates the US soldiers who died in the Aisne–Marne Salient in 1918. Visitors can learn about the battles from the orientation map on the monument and there's a very good new visitor centre too.

Aisne–Marne American Cemetery (At the entrance of Belleau, see below; ☎ 03 23 70 70 90; ⊕ 09.00–17.00 daily; free entry) The cemetery sits at the foot of the famous Belleau Wood battlefield and contains the graves of 2,289 US soldiers, most of whom fought in the vicinity during the summer of 1918.

Musée de la Mémoire de Belleau 1914–1918 (Pl du Général Pershing, Belleau; ☎ 03 23 82 03 63; w museedebelleau.com; ⊕ 8 May–11 Nov 10.00–12.30 & 13.30–17.30 Thur–Mon; free entry) This intriguing museum of memorabilia has a special significance for the US Marine Corps who fought in the Battle of Belleau Wood and suffered heavy losses. The visitor centre features an array of interpretative exhibits and multimedia displays aimed at putting the US role in World War I in perspective.

Oise–Aisne American Cemetery (1 mile east of Fère-en-Tardenois; w abmc.gov/Oise-Aisne; ⊕ 09.00–17.00 daily; free entry) Contains the remains of 6,013 American soldiers who lost their lives while fighting in the vicinity. Their headstones rise along a gentle slope to the curved colonnade, flanked by a chapel and map room at the far end. The latter contains an engraved map portraying the military operations in the region during 1918.

OISE

Oise is the third *département* to make up the Picardy region. In summer 1914, German troops flooded through here to try and take Paris, although they would be pushed back during the First Battle of the Marne (see box, page 104).

On 11 November 1918, French, British and German commanders met in a forest east of the town of **Compiègne** that could be reached by rail; they gathered in this secretive spot to sign the Armistice ending World War I. The Clairière de l'Armistice, or Clairière de Rethondes, therefore became one of the most hallowed of places to the people of France and many others. After a stint in Paris, the railway carriage in which the meeting occurred was moved back to Compiègne Forest in 1920. A memorial museum opened there so visitors could see the carriage and learn about the Armistice.

However, at the beginning of World War II, following the lightning German occupation of France in 1940, Hitler rushed to the exact same spot in the forest of Compiègne to humiliate the French with the signing of a new Armistice heralding Germany's crushing domination of the country. The memorial museum was erased and the Führer had the historic railway carriage taken to Berlin, where it would be destroyed on Hitler's orders in 1945.

However, a similar wagon, which was rebuilt after World War II, stands in the much-modernised **Memorial de L'Armistice** (Rte de Soissons, 60200 Compiegne; ☎ 03 44 85 14 18; w armistice-museum.com; ⊕ Jan–Nov 10.00–18.00 daily, last admission 17.30; Dec 10.00–17.30 daily, last admission 16.45; adult/7–18 €7/5).

11

Marne, Champagne and Verdun

Along with Flanders and Picardy, an arc of land stretching east from Paris via Reims to Verdun became another of the most terrible theatres of conflict throughout World War I. This arc notably included sections of the Marne and Meuse valleys.

The name of the Marne is indelibly associated with the heroic defence of Paris from invasion in September 1914, and the saving of France from very swift capitulation to Germany. As to Verdun on the Meuse, it has the same resonance for the French as the name of the Somme for Britain and the Commonwealth, witnessing as it did another of the most destructive battles in the history of humanity.

Visiting these parts in the context of World War I, the pleasures of bubbly Champagne seem far removed, yet some uplifting war tales stand out, such as the celebrated story of Paris taxi drivers ferrying soldiers to the First Battle of the Marne, a small but psychologically important part of the war effort. Soldiers of many different nationalities, including British, Commonwealth and American troops, fought in battles from the Marne to the Meuse, and of course the losses for the Germans would be immense.

MEAUX

MUSEUM OF THE GREAT WAR (MUSÉE DE LA GRANDE GUERRE) (*Rue Lazare Ponticelli, Meaux;* \ *01 60 32 14 18;* w *museedelagrandeguerre.eu;* ⏱ *09.30–18.00 Mon & Wed– Sun, closed 15 Aug–1 Sep; adult/seniors & students/under 26s/under 8s €10/7/5/free*) Europe's biggest World War I museum is located above the town of Meaux northeast of Paris and close to some of the main locations of fighting in the early stages of the First Battle of the Marne. It is a rich curtain-raiser to exploring the wide-ranging social upheavals brought about by the war to end all wars. Inaugurated appropriately at 11.00 on 11 November 2011, it focuses on the personal lives of those who took part, as well as the military or political issues. At its heart is a collection of 50,000 objects collected over a period of 40 years by photographer Jean-Pierre Verney and bought by the regional councils, who also agreed to provide a massive high-tech museum to house the collection. These items include uniforms, prosthetic limbs, barbed wire, gas masks and a host of other wartime paraphernalia. One gallery shows objects carved and shaped in the trenches, from erotic reliefs cut into the brass casings of shells to bullets turned into salt shakers. One section focuses in detail on the different stages of the First Battle of the Marne. There are two routes through the museum: the first takes 90 minutes, the other either a half or full day. Allow around 75 minutes for an all-round look at the conflict, followed perhaps by a themed tour, taking from a half- to a full-day visit, to explore specific aspects of the conflict. These include women at war, daily life in the trenches, tactics and the role of the USA, complete with a reconstruction of an American camp.

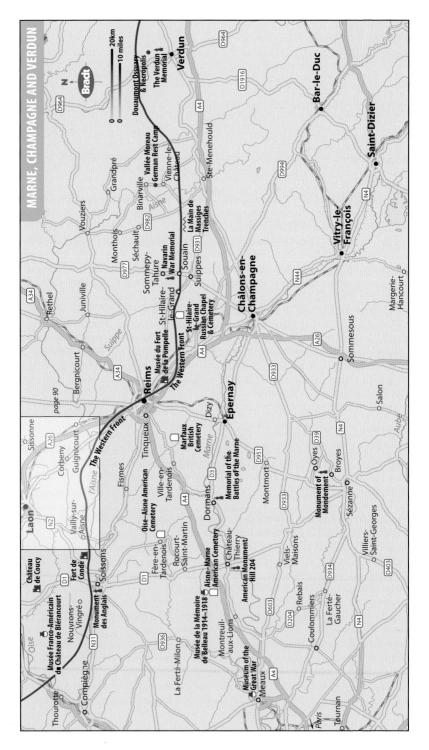

Douaumont Ossuary & Necropolis
The Verdun Memorial
Verdun

D964

D1916

D964

0 — 20km
0 — 10 miles

N

Bradt

Grandpré

Binarville
Vallée Moreau
German Rest Camp
Vienne-le-Château

Bar-le-Duc

Vouziers

Séchault

Monthois

Aisne

D982

Sommepy-
Tahure

D977

St-Hilaire-
le-Grand

La Main de
Massiges
Trenches
O Navarin
War Memorial

Ste-Menehould

Saint-Dizier

Rethel

A34

Souain

Suippes

D994

Vitry-le-
François

Juniville

D931

**Châlons-en-
Champagne**

N4

St-Hilaire-
le-Grand
Russian Chapel
& Cemetery

A4

Margerie-
Hancourt

Suippe

Bergnicourt

Musée du Fort
de la Pompelle

A34

N44

A26

Sommesous

page 90

Reims

The Western Front

Dizy

Sissonne

A26

D933

Salon

Corbeny

Guignicourt

Tinqueux

Marfaux
British
Cemetery

Epernay

Laon

N2

Vailly-sur-
Aisne

The Western Front

l'Aisne

Fismes

Marne

Ville-en-
Tardenois

Memorial of the
Battles of the Marne

D951

Montmort

Aube

D39

N4

Monument of
O Oyes

Broyes

Château
de Coucy

D1

Oise

Fort de
Condé

Soissons

D1

Oise-Aisne American
Cemetery

A4

Dormans
D3

D933

Mondement

Sézanne

Villiers-
Saint-Georges

Monument Franco-Américain
du Château de Blérancourt

Nouvrons-
Vingréo

Monument
des Anglais

N31

Fère-en-
Tardenois

Rocourt-
Saint-Martin

Château-
Thierry

Viels-
Maisons

D603

Rebais

La Ferté-
Gaucher

D934

D403

Thourotte

D936

Musée de la Mémoire
de Belleau 1914–1918

Aisne–Marne
American Cemetery

American Monument/
Hill 204

D204

Coulommiers

N4

La Ferté-
Milon

Montreuil-
aux-Lions

A4

D603

O Compiègne

Museum of the
Great War

Meaux

Tournan

Paris

La Main de Massiges Trenches (HL/S)

REIMS

The major historic city of Reims, on the Vesle River north of the Marne Valley, contains one of the most important medieval cathedrals in France, while celebrated Champagne vineyards lie close by. However, at the start of World War I, the town found itself on the route of German forces sweeping down from Belgium and the Ardennes towards Paris, 129km (80 miles) away. Germans occupied the city from 4 to 13 September 1914. Thanks to the counteroffensive of the First Battle of the Marne, the French Army quickly retook Reims, but German troops then stationed themselves in forts surrounding the town. As a result, the city suffered devastating bombardments for 3½ years. The cathedral alone was hit by almost 300 shells. Reims lay 60% in ruins by the conflict's end, and 740 civilians had lost their lives.

GETTING THERE AND AWAY From Calais **by car**, follow the E15/A25 south to Arras and then pick up the E17/A26 to Reims (*272km; approx 2hrs 30mins*). By **train**, take the TGV, which departs regularly from Paris Gare de L'Est (*45mins*).

TOURIST INFORMATION

Reims Tourist Office 6 Rue Rockefeller, 51100 Reims; ☏ 0821 61 01 60 (€0.11/min); w reims-tourisme.com

Regional Tourist Information w tourisme-en-champagne.co.uk

WHAT TO SEE AND DO

La Main de Massiges Trenches (*South of Reims; signposted from the village of Massiges;* w *lamaindemassiges.com; free entrance is only for private individuals & small groups Mar–Nov 09.00–18.00, guided tours are possible with booking*) This is a mind-boggling network of trenches and fortifications on private land littered with the likes of roots, stakes and barbed wire left over from the fierce trench warfare that took place here (during the two Battles of Champagne) between September 1915 and September 1918, with trenches changing hands between enemies several times. Seven bodies – six French soldiers and one German – were discovered in 2012 and 2013, which have since been buried in local military cemeteries, although this number may well have risen.

Marne 14–18 Interpretation Centre (*4 Ruelle Bayard, Suippes;* 03 26 68 24 09; w *marne14-18.fr;* Feb–Jun & Sep–Nov 13.00–18.00 Tue, Thu–Fri & Sun; Jul–Aug 10.00–18.00 Tue, Thu–Fri & Sun; adult/6–18/under 6s €6.50/3/free) Located on the former Front, this is another museum that takes an interactive dip into the daily lives of soldiers and civilians through masses of original photos and first-hand accounts from soldiers. Use your fingerprint to get a guide, male or female, who will accompany you throughout the visit.

Vallée Moreau German Rest Camp (*Route 63, between Vienne-le-Château & Binarville;* 03 26 60 49 40; Jan–May & Oct–Dec 09.00–noon Sat; Jul–Sep 09.00–noon Sat & 14.00–17.00 Sun; guided tour adult/child €8.50/4.50) This fascinating collection of trenches, tunnels and buildings has been slowly restored by the Franco-German Committee since 1966. The rest camp was designed to hold several hundred 'off-duty' soldiers, and visitors can experience the daily life of the troops. Interestingly, when construction started in 1915 it was supervised by a young junior officer called Rommel – the future World War II Field Marshal.

Navarin War Memorial (*D977, between Souain & Sommepy-Tahure;* 03 26 66 82 32; memorial: daily; chapel: mid-Mar–late Sep 14.00–18.00 Fri & Sat, 10.00–noon & 14.00–18.00 Sun & bank holidays; 11 Nov 10.00–noon & 14.00–16.00; free entry) Located in the heart of the Champagne battlefields and topped by a sculpture depicting three soldiers, this monument commemorates the fighting of October 1914 and September 1915. The surrounding land still bears the scars of heavy conflict.

Musée du Fort de la Pompelle (*5km from Reims on the RN44 towards Châlons-en-Champagne;* 03 26 49 11 85; w *musees-reims.fr/fr/musees/musee-du-fort-de-la-pompelle;* 10.00–18.00 Tue–Sun; adult/concession/under18s €5.50/3.30/free) This fort was built in 1880 as one of a ring of defence points around Reims. During four years of heavy shelling in World War I, it was the only citadel around the city to remain in the hands of the Allied forces (French and Russian troops). Once a monument that symbolised the city's resistance against the invaders, the fort became a war museum housing a rich collection of artefacts. It now contains an important military collection, featuring the unique Friese collection of 560 items of headgear that belonged to the German Imperial Army.

THE BATTLE OF THE MARNE

The pivotal **First Battle of the Marne** was fought between 5 and 9 September 1914. The Germans were nearing the outskirts of Paris in their bid to occupy France, but six French armies and one British regiment engaged them in battle along a wide section of the Marne River and beyond and won. The Germans were forced to retreat to the northeast and abandon their push on Paris – the delay lost them their swift victory over France and set the stage for four years of trench warfare.

The **Second Battle of the Marne** took place between 15 July and 5 August 1918 and was the last major German offensive on the Front during World War I. German forces attacked the French around Reims. However, when American troops and a British Corps joined the French, the Germans were overwhelmed. The German defeat marked the start of a relentless Allied advance that culminated in the Armistice being signed about 100 days later.

La Pompelle Fort museum features a unique collection of German imperial army headgear (APL/A)

Saint-Hilaire-le-Grand Russian Chapel and Cemetery (*D21, L'Espérance;* ⊕ *15 Apr–15 Nov 14.00–18.00 daily but check first; free entry*) This isolated chapel on the Aubérive road is dedicated to the 6,100 Russian soldiers among those sent over by the Tsar who died in France. The adjacent cemetery is the final resting place for around 1,000 of them. After the October Revolution in 1917 most Russian troops became 'voluntary workers', while those who refused were sent to camps in Algeria and 2,000 men went on serving in the Moroccan Division. A monument to the Russian 2nd Special Regiment stands opposite the cemetery.

Memorial of the Battles of the Marne, Dormans (*Av des Victoires, Dormans;* ℂ *03 26 59 14 18;* w *cheminsdememoire.gouv.fr/en/memorial-battles-marne-dormans;* ⊕ *1 Apr–11 Nov 14.30–18.00 Mon–Sat, 10.00–noon Sun; free entry, €2 for a 45min guided tour*) One of France's four French national memorials, it looks out over vineyards and the Marne River, and commemorates the two Battles of the Marne, which occured in 1914 and 1918. The memorial comprises a crypt, chapel and ossuary containing the remains of over 1,000 soldiers of mixed nationalities.

Monument of Mondement (*D45, between Oyes & Broyes;* w *mondement1914. asso.fr/english;* ⊕ *monument: daily; museum: Jun–Sep 15.00–18.00 Sun*) This monument in the hamlet of Mondement-Montgivroux commemorates the First Battle of the Marne and is located at a strategic point in the conflict. The accompanying Mondement History Museum is housed in the former village school.

Marfaux British Cemetery (*D386, between Dormans & Reims;* ⊕ *daily; free entry*) This Commonwealth cemetery contains the graves of 1,114 British soldiers, of which 789 have been identified, and commemorates, by name, ten of the 15 casualties of the New Zealanders Cyclist Battalion who fell in July 1918.

The battlefield at Verdun, still marked by shell holes (CT/TGV)

VERDUN

The name of Verdun, a significant small city on the Meuse River in the northeastern French region of Lorraine, is inextricably linked with one of the most appalling wars of attrition ever pursued by opposing forces. The Battle of Verdun in 1916 (see box, opposite) became the longest battle of World War I. Over 300,000 French and German soldiers died and over 400,000 were wounded within an area of only 20km². The so-called Red Zone, the area at the heart of the conflict, still bears its terrible scars.

GETTING THERE AND AWAY From Reims **by car**, follow the E17/A4 southeast towards Châlons-en-Champagne, then pick up the E50/A4 near La Veuve (*121km; approx 1hr 15mins*).

TOURIST INFORMATION

Verdun Tourist Office Place de la Nation; \ 03 29 86 14 18; w en.tourisme-verdun.com; ⊕ Jan 09.00–noon & 14.00–17.00 Mon–Sat; Feb–Mar & Oct–Nov 09.00–noon & 13.30–17.30 Mon–Sat, 09.00–13.00 Sun; Apr–Sep 09.00–12.30 & 13.30–18.00 Mon–Sat, 10.00–12.30 & 13.30–17.00 Sun; Dec 09.00–noon & 14.00–17.00 Mon–Sat, 09.00–13.00 Sun

> ### MEUSE–ARGONNE OFFENSIVE
>
> On the morning of 26 September 1918, Allied tanks and infantry advanced against German positions in the Argonne Forest in what would become the largest battle in American military history. With US General John J Pershing in command and over one million US troops participating, it was also the largest American-run offensive of the war. The battle ended on 11 November 1918 after the signing of the Armistice, bringing World War I to a close.

Fought over the course of ten months, between 21 February and 18 December 1916, the Battle of Verdun was initiated by the Germans, who wanted to deal the Allies on the Western Front a crushing blow by capturing the Meuse Heights and the French-held fortified town of Verdun – a vital gateway town on the way to Paris. It was arguably the most influential battle of World War I.

On 21 February, the Germans began by bombarding French lines for over 21 hours. Progress was slow, but four days later they captured Douaumont Fortress. After some early gains in territory by the Germans, however, fierce retaliations by the French led the battle into a bloody stalemate, and the conflict became a devastating battle of wills – fighting for fighting's sake over an area of just 20km^2 with a few metres being gained and then lost.

Calculations from historical documents suggest that there were over 70,000 casualties for each month of fighting, with approximately 542,000 French and 434,000 German casualties – close to a million casualties in total – making it one of the longest and costliest battles in human history. Historians estimate that 40 million artillery rounds were expended during the battle. The German defeat marked the start of a relentless Allied advance that culminated in the Armistice being signed about 100 days later.

WHAT TO SEE AND DO
Underground Citadel (Citadelle Souterraine) (*Av du Soldat Inconnu;* \03 29 84 84 42; w *citadelle-souterraine-verdun.fr;* ⊕ *Feb & Dec 09.30–17.00 daily; Mar & Nov 09.30–17.30 daily; Apr–Jun & Sep–Oct 09.00–18.00 daily; Jul–Aug 09.00–19.00 daily; adult/8–16/family of 4 €15/8/40, children under 8 not permitted*) Dug between 1886 and 1893, these galleries depict the lives of French soldiers who were stationed here. Nowadays, visitors board a small train to see some of them (advanced booking required, maximum 9 people per carriage, departs every 6 mins). Throughout the visit, realistic tableaux illustrate the everyday life of soldiers during the Battle of Verdun. At the end of the visit a tableau depicts the selection of the body of the Unknown Soldier (see box, page 51).

Underground Citadel, Verdun (CT/TGV)

The Verdun Memorial (*1 Av du Corps Européen, 55100 Fleury-devant-Douaumont;* \03 29 88 19 16; w *memorial-verdun.fr;* ⊕ *4 Feb–14 Ap & 18 Sep–31 Dec 09.30–17.30 daily; 15 Apr–17 Sep 09.30–18.30 daily; adult/concession/family of 3 €12/7.50/27, €6 for each additional child 8–18; ask about combined ticket discounts with Fort de Douaumont & Fort de Vaux*) Lying at the heart of the

battlefield, some 4km from Verdun, this memorial is a 21st-century multimedia reflection of the massacre that took place.

During a 90-minute visit, an audio-visual display measuring more than 1,000ft^2 utilises archive images and artistic interpretations to provide a realistic demonstration of not only the soldiers' combative experiences, but also the violence of the battle – and the home fronts from both the French and German angle. More than 2,000 objects and photos bear testament to the French and German people tormented by conflict. The display ends in a tranquil setting, bathed in soft light, ideal for reflection and contemplation: look out on the landscape of the battlefield, or perhaps peruse supplementary materials at the digital kiosks.

The memorial also has a **Documentation Centre**: to make a research appointment contact Isabelle Bergot-Remy (e *isabelle.bergot-remy@memorial-verdun.fr;* ⊕ *09.30–noon & 14.00–17.00 Mon–Fri*).

Douaumont Ossuary and Necropolis (*55100 Douaumont;* ✆ *03 29 84 54 81;* w *verdun-douaumont.com;* ⊕ *Feb 09.00–noon & 14.00–17.00 Mon–Fri, 14.00–17.00 Sat–Sun; Mar 09.00–noon & 14.00–17.30 Mon–Fri, 10.00–noon & 14.00–17.30 Sat–Sun; Apr–Jun 09.00–18.00 Mon–Fri, 10.00–18.00 Sat–Sun; Jul–Aug 09.00–18.30 daily; Sep 09.00–18.00 Mon–Fri, 10.00–18.00 Sat–Sun; Oct 09.00–18.00 Mon–Fri, 10.00–17.30 Sat–Sun; Nov 09.00–noon & 14.00–17.00 Mon–Sat, 10.00–noon & 14.00–17.00 Sat–Sun; Dec 14.00–17.00; adult/child (8–16) €7/3*) Officially opened by President Albert Lebrun on 7 August 1932, the Douaumont Ossuary contains the remains of 130,000 unknown French and German soldiers who died at the Battle of Verdun. The 137m-long cloister has tombs in pink granite with bones collected from all 36 areas of the battlefield. With 204 steps, the 46m-high tower contains a war museum in the middle. Unveiled on 29 June 1929, the necropolis stretches out in front of the ossuary with orderly rows of 15,000 crosses, the largest French necropolis of the Verdun battlefield and an immensely humbling sight. As with so many similar memorials, an audio-visual presentation, *Verdun Men of Mud*, is a timely reminder of the folly of war and the need for reconciliation and peace.

Douaumont Ossuary (CT/TGV)

Appendix

FURTHER INFORMATION

BOOKS There are hundreds of history books that cover the four-year war. These are a collection of the most authoritative and/or accessible.

Howard, Michael *The First World War: A Very Short Introduction* Oxford University Press, 2007. Ideal, quick read to understand the basics.

Patch, Harry *The Last Fighting Tommy* Bloomsbury, 2013. A frank account of the horrors of war. Harry died in 2009 at the age of 111 – the last surviving soldier of World War I.

Paxman, Jeremy *Great Britain's Great War* Viking, 2013. Brings to life what war was like for everyone, from the politicians and Tommies to wives and nurses.

Stevenson, David *1914–1918: The History of the First World War* Penguin, 2012. Very thorough coverage written by London School of Economics' International History Professor.

Strachan, Hew *The First World War* Free Press, 2006. Academic work by one of the world's leading World War I experts.

Taylor, A J P *The First World War: An Illustrated History* Penguin Books, 1974. This classic textbook guide to World War I is concise, but Taylor's style is rather dry in places and his opinions biased and largely out of date now. However, the numerous photos and diagrams still make it a worthwhile read.

WEBSITES

World War I
- w **greatwar.co.uk**
- w **flandersfields1418.com**
- w **memoire-pas-de-calais.com**
- w **visit-somme.com/great-war/remembrance-trail**

Tourist information
- w **jaimelaisne.com** (Aisne)
- w **lilletourism.com** (Lille)
- w **pas-de-calais.com** (Pas-de-Calais)
- w **somme-battlefields.com** (Somme)
- w **toerismeieper.be** (Ypres)
- w **tourisme-nord.com** (Le Nord)
- w **visitflanders.co.uk** (Flanders)
- w **visitmons.co.uk** (Mons)

Giving something back
- w **cwgc.org** The Commonwealth War Graves Commission maintain memorials & graveyards across France & Belgium.
- w **nfassociation.org** The Not Forgotten Association provides recreation for wounded, injured or sick ex-servicemen & women.

Travel
- w **delijn.be** Public transport network in Flanders
- w **sncf-connect.com** Booking website for all train travel in France
- w **belgiantrain.be** Booking website for all train travel in & around Belgium

GLOSSARY

ANZAC	Australian and New Zealand Army Corps
British Expeditionary Force	British Army deployed to the Front

JOIN

THE TRAVEL CLUB

THE MEMBERSHIP CLUB FOR SERIOUS TRAVELLERS
FROM BRADT GUIDES

Be inspired
Free books and exclusive
insider travel tips
and inspiration

Save money
Special offers and
discounts from our
favourite travel brands

Plan the trip
of a lifetime
Access our exclusive concierge
service and have a bespoke
itinerary created for you
by a Bradt author

Join here:
bradtguides.com/travelclub

Membership levels to suit all budgets

Bradt GUIDES

TRAVEL TAKEN SERIOUSLY

Are you looking for a unique and immersive walking holiday or cycling trip? The **Western Front Way** is a story-led, self guided trail along the lines of the First World War that will capture your imagination as you go.

- Annual Subscriptions
- Navigate & track progress
- Pre-purchase examples available
- Stories, letters and audio as you go
- In-app accommodation booking system
- Further resources to events and local information
- Mapped as 'stages' to suit time, destination and ability
- Mini-break, long weekend and full itineraries available

Whether you are looking for a once-in-a-lifetime experience, a long distance achievement, a weekend with a historical twist, or a journey of self-discovery, the Western Front Way is a remarkable place.

www.thewesternfrontway.com

Index

INDEX OF ADVERTISERS